The Silver Archive #1A
SAPPHIRE & STEEL
Assignments One and Two

By David and Lesley McIntee

THE SILVER ARCHIVE

SAPPHIRE AND STEEL - ASSIGNMENTS ONE AND TWO

ISBN: 9781909031760

Published by Obverse Books, Edinburgh

Range Editor: Stuart Douglas
Cover Design: Cody Schell

First edition: August 2018
10 9 8 7 6 5 4 3 2 1

A CIP catalogue record for this title is available from the British Library.

For Lesley's father, William Rhodes, and his interest in mathematics and clocks.

2018 Titles

The Silver Archive #1a: **Sapphire & Steel** *Assignments 1 & 2*

- David and Lesley McIntee

The Silver Archive #1b: **Sapphire & Steel** *Assignments 3 & 4*

- Cody Schell

The Silver Archive #1c: **Sapphire & Steel** *Assignments 5 & 6*

- James Cooray Smith

The Silver Archive #02: **Stranger Things**: *Season 1*

- Paul Driscoll

The Silver Archive #03: **The Strange World of Gurney Slade**

- Andrew Hickey

The Silver Archive #04: **Buffy the Vampire Slayer**: *Innocence*

- Jon Arnold

CONTENTS

OVERVIEW — Assignment One

Serial Title: Assignment One
Writer: P.J. Hammond
Director: Shaun O'Riordan

Original UK Transmission Dates: 10 July 1979
                                           12 July 1979
                                           17 July 1979
                                           19 July 1979
  24 July 1979
  26 July 1979

Running Times: Episode 1: 25m 40s
Episode 2: 24m 30s
Episode 3: 24m 00s
Episode 4: 25m 40s
Episode 5: 24m 40s
Episode 6: 24m 40s

UK Viewing Figures: Episode 1: 23%
Episode 2: 22%
Episode 3: 22%
Episode 4: 22%
Episode 5: 22%
Episode 6: 21%

[As percentage of the viewing audience]

Regular cast: Joanna Lumley (Sapphire), David McCallum (Steel)

Guest Cast: Steven O'Shea (Rob), Tamasin Bridge (Helen), Val Pringle (Lead), Felicity Harrison (Mother), John Golightly (Father), Charles Pemberton (Policeman), Ronald Goodale (Countryman)

Antagonists: Unspecified creatures from within the 'corridor' that is Time, and "Visual Refractions" (Ghosts of Roundhead soldiers and a plague-ridden Countryman)

Critical Responses:
'The atmosphere they conjure up really is outstanding, though. It's a simple setting, but lonely and spooky in all the right ways. Frankly I wouldn't expect even a feature film to be able to improve on what's being conjured up here. Apparently, this was a low-budget series, which makes its achievements all the more impressive.'

[Finn Clark, 'Sapphire and Steel: Assignment 1', *Finn Clark's Reviews*, August 2010]

'The production budget of Sapphire and Steel leaves a lot to be desired. Sets are minimal and appear as if they were borrowed from other productions being filmed at the same time. The main villains of the story are circles of light seemingly projected by flashlights off camera. To the best of my knowledge even the British series Dr. Who, which was renowned for its cheap rubber-suited monsters and villains, never stooped so low as to resort to flashlights for its characters.'

[Steve Phillips, 'Sapphire and Steel', *Andy's Anachronisms -- Time Travel Television Reviews*, July 2003]

OVERVIEW — Assignment Two

Serial Title: Assignment Two
Writer: P.J. Hammond
Directors: Shaun O'Riordan (Except Episodes 5 & 6) and David Foster (except Episode 8)

Original UK Transmission Dates: 31 July 1979
2 August 1979
7 August 1979
9 August 1979
30 October 1979
1 November 1979
6 November 1979
8 November 1979

Running Times: Episode 1: 27m 00s
Episode 2: 25m 40s
Episode 3: 24m 50s
Episode 4: 25m 30s
Episode 5: 27m 40s
Episode 6: 25m 40s
Episode 7: 24m 50s
Episode 8: 25m 30s

UK Viewing Figures: Episode 1: 22%
Episode 2: 21%
Episode 3: 18%
Episode 4: 20%
Episode 5: 19%
Episode 6: 20%
Episode 7: 19%
Episode 8: 20%

[As percentage of the viewing audience]

Regular cast: Joanna Lumley (Sapphire), David McCallum (Steel)

Guest Cast: Gerald James (George Tully), Tom Kelly (Pvt. Sam Pearce), David Woodcock (Submariner/voices), David Cann (Pilot/voices)

Antagonists: The Darkness.

Critical Responses:

'With just a handful of sets it achieves an extraordinary sense of claustrophobia, melancholy and at times stark terror. It is an exceptionally clever and unconventional ghost story, of ghosts who have been cheated.'

['Sapphire and Steel, Assignments One to Four', *Cult TV Lounge*]

'Sapphire & Steel's finest hour...a classic piece of television.'

[Richard Callaghan, *Assigned! The Unofficial and Unauthorised Guide to Sapphire & Steel*]

INTRODUCTION: SAPPHIRE AND STEEL HAVE BEEN ASSIGNED

> All irregularities will be handled by the forces controlling each dimension. Transuranic heavy elements may not be used where there is life. Medium atomic weights are available: Gold, Lead, Copper, Jet, Diamond, Radium, Sapphire, Silver and Steel. Sapphire and Steel have been assigned.

Thus opens the first episode of this seminal otherworldly TV series. There are many reasons for using 'otherworldly' as a descriptor, and one of them would be because the series transcends any other. Is it science fiction? Well, some of its themes are, but it sits equally well in the genres of horror, fantasy, and psychological drama. It's not a children's series but started as one; everything about it is slightly other than it appears to be, and other than the labels that culture likes to apply to creative works, whether in the 1970s or today.

That opening narration seems simple enough, to equate the lead characters with atomic elements. It sounds science-fiction-ish, yet this, from the very beginning, is an illusion. These words are going to mean something other than what they mean in our world. They may be called elements, but, as we'll see, this isn't quite right. There's a slightly longer, similar, word, for which 'elements' is but a shorthand here.

Yet in the sense of atoms being building blocks, the basic elements that form the structure of matter are a fitting comparison, because we were about to meet archetypes who represent the alchemy of storytelling and the continuance of knowledge through history. Stories have always conveyed knowledge and memory; it's one of the reasons why it's very important that history happens in the right order, as the show would seem to agree.

What of the 'forces controlling each dimension?' The idea of dimensions as different levels of reality is a long-established science fiction trope, in the form of parallel or mirror universes, but the 1970s was also the decade in which folklorists and Ufologists came together in common purpose, to suggest that other-worldly beings, whether aliens, Faeries, or element spirits such as Djinn or poltergeists, originated from layers of dimensions in our own world, but beyond the four which we can normally perceive.

The prime mover in advancing this theory was Jacques Vallée, a French computer scientist, in his 1968 book *Passport to Magonia*. In this book he put forth the idea that many elements of UFO sightings were similar to descriptive elements in historical reports for Faeries, incubi, the Blessed Virgin Mary and the like. In fact, Vallée became so well known that Francois Truffaut's character, Claude LaCombe, in the movie *Close Encounters of The Third Kind* (1977) was based upon him[1].

At the same time, the emerging science of quantum mechanics was postulating that the universe did in fact have more than four dimensions of measurement, and that we could not perceive the others. It's simple enough to see how it could be hinted at that ghosts, spirits, and other beings could be hidden in those dimensions, or for the dimensions to be used as a means of concealment or transition. In this respect, **Sapphire & Steel** was well up to date with what was then brand new thinking, albeit not widely known in the public or media consciousness. These were

---

[1] Umland, Samuel J, and Rebecca Umland, *The Use of Arthurian Legend in Hollywood Film: From Connecticut Yankees to Fisher Kings*, p.27

very niche subjects, of interest and awareness to only Forteans, folklorists, Ufologists, and a small subset of physicists and mathematicians, but – whether deliberately or coincidentally – the series fitted tonally very well with the developments of the time in this rather esoteric field of research.

This brings us back to that E-word: Elements (or Elementals). It's a common magical belief in many cultures that names have meaning, and words have power. One should, in Celtic myth, never give one's name to one of the Fair Folk, because the ownership of that word can be transferred, giving over control of what it represents.

We can safely assume that Sapphire, Steel, Lead and Silver are not the agents' real names. By calling something out of the shadows and naming it, so we hope to neutralise it – that's very old magical, irrational, thinking, though it mirrors scientific thought which says that we change the state of things simply by observing them. And, as a species, we can never resist naming anything we can observe.

The choice of the characters' names is clearly meant to create among the audience certain expectations of their personalities, which can later be played upon or challenged. Steel, who dresses in sombre grey is expected to be humourless and stern. Cold and hard, even, resilient to attack, but also sharp and cutting.

'Cold steel' evokes the warrior and the weapon, ruthless and intractable, who does not break – though, of course, when steel is repeatedly heated and cooled, when steel blades don't have enough flex (if the proportion of carbon isn't high enough), they can and do snap. We see this in *Assignment One*, when his insistence on dropping his temperature renders Steel vulnerable and in need of rescue. He also ignores Sapphire's advice in *Assignment Two*, refusing to be flexible in his intent to have a face to face meeting with the Darkness, and so walks straight into a trap.

In many ways, Steel's strengths are in fact also his weaknesses, reflecting both the resilient and brittle aspects of his metallic nature. Yes, he can lower his temperature to absolute zero – but he needs a chemical reaction and the assistance of Lead to warm back up, because he can't do it himself. This demonstration that he needs others – this emphasis on teamwork – to perform best is an important one to the young viewers of the first story.

This also correctly reflects how alloys and mixing elements works in the physical world; combining lead with steel makes it more machine-workable, though it doesn't affect the steel's tensile strength. If you want to change the temperature at which a metal can be worked, mixing it with others is a good way to do it.

Sapphire, on the other hand, like a jewel, scintillates in appearance, wit and conversation, constantly revealing new facets and new talents in a variety of settings. Applying anthropomorphism of this kind to inanimate objects is not new, in fact is part of a general Western cultural awareness of, and fascination with, the Other and the Otherworldly.

As far back as a couple of centuries BCE, Graeco-Roman alchemists, and later the Arabs of the 7th Century onwards, and then the alchemists of the medieval and Renaissance eras, codified their ideas in texts which personified the metals as agents in a drama of transformation. The sequence of transformation, usually runs as follows: lead, tin, iron, copper, silver, gold, and finally the 'philosopher's stone.' This last was not an actual stone – as in the Harry Potter novel – but a type of metal with the ability to transform all other metals by use of the smallest part of it. Or, if you prefer, transforming the alchemist's psyche and understanding by means of knowledge, history, and types of thought.

Pictorial allegory and references to classical myth were used both to illustrate these alchemical secrets to adepts, and to conceal their meanings from unsympathetic authorities and anyone else. Illustrated alchemical allegories feature antagonisms, relationships, duels and even marriages leading to births among the anthropomorphised metals and their astronomical and mythological representatives.

All the alchemical elements have revealing appearances and physical characteristics which relate to their real-world chemical properties. Mercury, quicksilver, is neither solid nor liquid, is fleet of foot and winged, and a has a trickster nature; lead is ponderous and heavy, silver is bright and noble, and so on.

This symbolism runs as an undercurrent of reference in much of European literature from Shakespeare to Joyce, and onward to Carl Jung, who saw in it a correlation to the symbols of the human unconscious thrown up in dreams. Sapphire and Steel are a perfect representation on screen of this sub-current of images and allegories (which Yeats called 'the golden chain'). Their partnership's repartee, occasional disputes, and its undertones of at least a close friendship, (though the word 'love' is used once) matches the alchemical metals as they are depicted in love and war in old texts. A balance is established between them, exactly as in the texts, where the relationships somehow remain distant and stilted, never acquiring an overtone of crudeness.

The metals in the texts do not only interact with one another. Many alchemical texts are medieval meta-texts, in which the alchemist himself has conversations with the metals and elements. These conversations become Platonic dialogues in which the alchemist tries to bend nature – the personae of the metals – to his will by persuasion, and nature inevitably resists and tries to persuade *him*. Steel, when talking to the mortal characters he meets in the series, has much in common with the Mercury of such dialogues. As the alchemical catalyst, Mercury is tricksy, querulous, rude, provocative, wily, cunning, know it all, and arrogant by turns. If this sounds like

Star Trek's Q, or certain incarnations of the Doctor in **Doctor Who**, as well as Steel, that's not likely to be a coincidence.

The exchanges between ghost hunter Tully and Steel in *Assignment Two* are especially reminiscent of dialogues between alchemists and Mercury. The latter intrudes on the former's area of expertise, a constant antagonism and point scoring ensues, and neither will give an inch; in Tully and Steel's case leaving Sapphire stuck in the middle. (Steel's point-scoring later leads to some serious errors of judgement, which place himself, Sapphire, and, of course, poor Tully, in extreme danger.)

Cold steel and the old adage about revenge being best served cold are not perhaps unrelated; can we discount an element of such very human and unpleasant emotion when Steel finally feeds Tully to the Darkness, in an ironic reversal of the alchemist's finally 'fixing' – and often, in so doing, 'killing' – his annoying metal interlocutor?

The pair clearly have a severe cultural and ideological clash. To Steel, human belief in a higher power is essentially irrelevant, and foolish, and Tully's use of Christian symbols and prayer at best a nuisance to his work. It is also very noticeable that when Tully appeals for deliverance to 'upstairs' it is the Darkness that lets him go as part of its plan. In the 1970s when Christian-oriented Religious Education was an often emphasised part of the Secondary School curriculum, **Sapphire & Steel** – in the person of Steel – is effectively exposing its viewers to a very rationally argued atheism, and to a universe of almost mystical physics and intellect. It can also be read as suggesting that a benevolent god does not seem to have a place in a universe where Time devours and makes deals for people's remaining years on Earth. And if God does not have a place, then what price morality? (A common but specious argument among the evangelically religious, who believe that morality derives from fear of a celestial Big Brother.)

Steel's morality in *Assignment Two* certainly seems to have some interesting variations from traditional modern western values. Literature and folklore have similarly used the characteristics of organic nature as jumping off points for anthropomorphised characters, as well as storylines that display such characters with that variation from the western norm: Elementals.

Common to both European and Middle Eastern folklore are stories of Elemental spirits who resemble and interact with mankind, be they called Elves, Faeries, Djinn, or whatever. These first appear in alchemy in the 16th Century work of the philosopher known as Paracelsus and evolve towards their more modern literary form in the works of the Romantics, and other 19th century writers, looking for inspiration in creating a 'new mythology' out of established elements. These Elemental beings inhabit and share traits with earth, air, water, and fire. Their folklore interacts with that of the Elves (Sidhe, shining ones, faery or in middle eastern terms Djinni), who can also form relationships, marry and even bear children to humans. These folkloric future staples of fantasy fiction are said by Lord Dunsany in *The Kith of The Elf-Folk* (1908) to recognise God, but to not have souls (though in some cases they can gain one by marrying a mortal), and their character is very much determined by the element they inhabit and are associated with.

The four elemental categories, based on Aristotelian elements, include the likes of gnomes and chthonic spirits in the Earth; and Kelpies, Selkies, and the eponymous Undine of German Romanticism in Water. Sylphs inhabit the air, and the Salamanders are Fire spirits. The latter category cannot, by their fiery nature, interact too closely with man, at least according to Paracelsus in *Ex Libro de Nymphis, Sylvanis, Pygmaeis, Salamandris, et Gigantibus*, published posthumously in 1566, who counts Man's spirit as the fifth element. As with the metals in alchemy – with an adjunct of medieval ideas of the humours, the essences of health or illness – these beings' physical characteristics are influenced by the element with which they're associated. Stoic, short and crafty for Earth

17

(hello to Tolkien's Dwarves), slim and ethereal and beautiful for the Sylphs of the Air, temperamental for the fire spirits, and so forth.

Elementals do not die like us, they are reabsorbed into their elements, and are, as such, immortal, though these myths feature individual distress when the elementals are rejected; a water spirit cursed three times on water for example, must leave its mortal lover.

The concept of a parallel being to ourselves, born out of the elements, but soulless, immortal and possibly amoral, hovers on the edge of those interchanges of myth, folklore, and psychology that characterise western literature, especially from the Romantic period onwards. it's not unreasonable to imagine that a wisp of the Sylph, the booming voice of the Earth spirit, or the wild contempt of the Kelpie luring men to their doom, may have influenced the personalities and appearances and actions of Sapphire and Steel and their fellows.

Sapphire's particular allure, the choice to cast her as a tall blonde, white woman is perhaps not just a pandering to the patriarchy and to received privileged western ideals of beauty of the 1970s. It is also the subliminal bequest of the western canon and everything of the older, oral, tradition of stories that has gone into it: the fascination with the otherworldly female, goddess, bride, seducer, mother, and nemesis. Such figures are necessarily problematic in our age with regard to gender and racial politics, but they are there among the archetypes.

Finally, in her briefly glimpsed red-headed persona, Sapphire echoes another otherworldly seducer, guardian, assister – and abductor of entirely willing mortals – popular in Celtic and European mythology, the Queen of the Elves. The Elves, subject of probably hundreds of tales in Irish and Scottish myth, as well as in Scandinavian and Eastern European, are notoriously amoral, by our modern Western standards, although they do sometimes punish indolence and reward honesty.

They also replace gold and food with leaves or stones, lead travellers astray, and, although they will sometimes seek mortal help (as in many tales of midwives carried off to assist at births), they are generally oblivious to mortal issues, or to the mental and physical cost to mortals who interact with them.

The ambivalence of these female characters in myth is a noted feature; they can also be sexually voracious and dominant, in a slightly transgressive – and in other cases threatening and warning – inversion of patriarchal norms traditionally imposed on the feminine. This is, on a safe level for a sometime children's series, visible in Sapphire's often precocious rejection of Steel's automatically assumed authority. It is only a flash but Sapphire should take her place among the feminist figures in SF.

One of the most prominent themes in the lore of Elves and their ilk is that mortals who encounter them or enter their realms do not return unchanged and that these risks have to do with both time and mortality[2].

The biggest clash of 'elvish' alien (or at least, non-human and non-western) and largely Christian morality occurs between Tully and Steel in *Assignment Two*. Tully's brand of Spiritualist Christianity, as noted above, is anathema to Steel's knowledge that the ghosts summoned by the Darkness are not redeemable, but his

---

[2] Thomas the Rhymer, for example, meets with the Faery queen in the hills of Eildon is abducted for seven years and returns with 'the tongue that can never lie', others, like the Irish poet Oisin, are gone for a moment to find hundreds of years have passed and they have very suddenly grown very old.

antagonism only drives Tully on and leads him to be manipulated by that force. The Darkness clearly manipulates both, feeding on their antagonism to put Steel in the position of having to use Tully's method – the séance – and paving the way for Sapphire's possession.

Tully's crisis of faith, and his relapse into cowardice, is a bleak point in the story, but not as bleak as where his principles lead him, a lamb to the slaughter. Again, this is no children's tale and a stark one for adults also.

Sapphire and Steel possess an odd bag of talents drawn from, and comparable to, characters from multiple points on the science fiction, speculative, and fantasy fiction spectrum. She is both empathic and telepathic, and exercises psychometry by 'reading' objects. She can freeze time locally, and even rewind it back, but her power is limited by some unknown facet of her nature and amounts to only a few hours' worth of time. Both she and Steel can influence matter at a distance.

Their abilities combine the traditional magus/magician with the alien telepath so familiar from science fiction. Those abilities are also a mixed bag of those claimed by a whole gaggle of New Age TV psychics such as Uri Geller (a frequent face on TV at the time). Remember, after all, that this series was contemporary with the ITV documentary series **Arthur C Clarke's Mysterious World** (1980). In mythic terms their appearance and disappearance at will, their power over men's minds – as when Steel convinces the local policeman that he's a family friend – and over inanimate objects, feeds also into the Magus myth, a subset of Joseph Campbell's hero myth or monomyth as subsequently developed by Professor Elsie Butler. The Magus is the direct ancestor of those marvellous men of science who appear as heroes, and anti-heroes, in 19th century literature (extending, of course, to our most famous Doctor). Patterning our two protagonists onto the Magus myth as Butler perceived it, the following correlations occur in the established stages of the traditional Magus story:

- *Undisclosed or mysterious parentage or origins.* Beyond the vague mention of Elements, we know little of either Steel or Sapphire. Are they born naturally? How old are they? Where do they come from? Who sends them? All we know – from *Assignment Three* – is that Steel has 'very positive' and 'impeccable' origins, but even he admits that these origins are 'inexpressible.'
- *Mysterious powers.* Our heroes have plenty of psychic ability on show.
- *Distant wanderings.* They seem to travel in both space and time, as they refer to historical cases such as the *Mary Celeste*[3], but also talk about humans as if they are but one species among many they have encountered. In *Assignment One*, Steel refers to needing 'a nursery rhyme and a human' to lure the entity they're up against, while in *Assignment Two*, when asked by Steel what the entities look like, she replies 'humans'. They are sent where there is life, not simply to Earth.
- *Tests, trials and tribulations.* These occur in each story and include possession, entrapment, physical threat or danger, physical pain, fear and isolation.
- *Death and rebirth* (or near misses). Steel's freezing himself almost solid and having to be brought back is an immediate example in *Assignment One*. Sapphire's being taken over by the Darkness in the second story makes it clear that both can be killed, or at least destroyed in some fashion[4].

---

[3] Not Marie Celeste, contrary to popular belief, as that name was coined by Sir Arthur Conan Doyle for his fictionalised telling of the tale in 'J. Habakuk Jephson's Statement', in 1884.

[4] 'Destroyed' being the term Sapphire uses when worrying about what the swan in *Assignment Three* might do to him.

- *A decisive magical battle*. This happens several times in *Assignment Two*, when both characters are displaced in time. They are also frozen into photographs by Shape in *Assignment Four*.
- *Death and defeat due to hubris*. The final story of the series springs to mind, and of course Tully's fate in *Assignment Two*, while presented as a victory for our heroes, is really a damage-limitation bodge-job resulting from Steel's arrogantly jumping to conclusions and acting upon them, before finding out what's really going on.

There are a couple of other types of entity that have influenced the creation of these two 'time agents' (as the original script intended them to be called). One which would have an influence throughout the series, always subverting the usual expectations, is the ghost.

Understandably, both Rob in *Assignment One* and then Tully in *Assignment Two* first assume that both Sapphire and Steel are ghosts, as they appear and disappear at will. Steel is clearly aware that this is a common line of approach for humans, as he makes ironic reference to it when he greets Tully with 'I come from the other side — the down platform.' That the pair are emphatically not ghosts is indicated by their characterisation of what humans call 'ghosts' as 'visual refractions' and by the clear use of the (unnamed in the serial) Stone Tape hypothesis[5] as an explanation for some of the phenomena they encounter.

The duo also have some very human characteristics, or at least can fake them perfectly well. They eat, (though it's unclear whether they require it, or get any nutrition from it), and are clearly not immune to physical harm, as mentioned when Sapphire is attacked by the 'ghost' Roundheads and threatened with execution. They

---

[5] The theory, most famously put forward in Nigel Kneale's 1972 teleplay **The Stone Tape**, that ghosts are recordings of past events made by the natural environment.

seem to have no *need* for sleep, though, as Steel states on the one occasion in which they do. Devoid of their supernatural abilities, their role falls into the realm of detectives and policing. After all what do police do but handle and sort irregularities and transgressions in the body social? The same principle applies here. Steel refers to his 'investigations' which are to be conducted and their first actions, once across the threshold of Rob and Helen's house, are to establish a framework of time and place of their 'crime' scene, and a motive. Witnesses are interviewed and suspects interrogated (starting with the child Helen in *Assignment One!*), usually with Sapphire as the Good Cop and Steel as the Bad Cop. They make alliances or enemies depending on their handling of the case and its current direction. As they investigate, it becomes clear that there are rules within which they operate, even if they bend or even break them. They also set up traps, plant or destroy evidence, negotiate for the rescue of hostages (such as Rob's parents), and so on.

As in the buddy-cop show, both make ironic jokes about previous cases) or about insider knowledge which they don't share with the 'civilians' – mortals who can be an out and out nuisance or a tolerated presence.

Although from a feminist perspective we should note that Sapphire's challenging of Steel's authority is progressive - as late as the 1990s in **The X-Files** the showrunners deliberately had Gillian Anderson's Scully positioned in shots a pace behind Mulder to reinforce the idea that she was the sidekick[6]. Here each takes the lead in turn and though she listens she doesn't always follow his lead.

---

[6] Anderson spoke about this in a January 2016 interview. https://www.thedailybeast.com/gillian-anderson-i-was-offered-half-duchovnys-pay-for-the-x-files-revival

Sapphire and Steel are pretty far from, say, **Starsky & Hutch**, but the tensions and loyalties between partners, their different skills sets, their hunches, their attitude to the 'perp' and their interactions, (friendly or otherwise) with colleagues from their own side, civilians, or higher authorities, let alone the perpetrators of trouble, means a lot of the characterisations tropes from the cop show applies here. We see it many times here, particularly in those moments where Sapphire gives a long-suffering smile at Steel's overbearing authority, goes off investigating on her own, takes charge, or makes Steel aware that his methods are unorthodox or they don't see eye to eye in treating witnesses.

Steel also gets tetchy at Lead and Silver's working on 'his' cases, whereas Sapphire welcomes them. One wonders if the series had gone on, whether we would have seen more of these tropes. Perhaps, covering the mythic and detective bases, one where Steel 'loses his badge' and is forced to live as a mortal. Sadly, in the context of a cop show, the ending, with the two detectives outwitted trapped by their Moriarty-like Nemeses, the Transient Beings (mortality itself, perhaps?) and imprisoned for eternity makes stark sense – and echoes their own entrapments of their opponents throughout the series, such as the patch-of-light entity in *Assignment One*, and perhaps (depending on your interpretation of what the Darkness actually does to people) Tully in *Assignment Two* as well.

Whether Elementals, cops, scientific anthropomorphisms, ghosts, or something else, Sapphire and Steel pattern themselves onto distinct and recognisable figures. With a nod to Jungian psychology, they are Archetypes.

The cunning man and the wise woman are long-established archetypes, appearing in order to lead lost travellers, to educate, or to protect. In terms of traditional monomyth, they are in some ways threshold guardians to the realm of adventure and the unknown.

Joseph Campbell, whose studies of the monomyth analysed the discrete units of western folklore, refers to the sometimes loathly, often frightening or intimidating, but always entirely fascinating, appearance of the guardian. He may well appear fearsome – after all he has come to take the hero over the threshold into manhood – but eventually he will prove of aid. In *Assignment One* in particular, intended for children's television, they play as the maternal and paternal – or at least in loco parentis – wise woman and cunning man.

One thing the audience is never allowed to forget is that, however strange the Operators (as they occasionally refer to themselves) appear to be, there is always a bigger fish. The opposition and threat may be mysterious and unknown, be it Time or unknowable creatures, but the thought that anything could be a danger to two such archetypal supernatural beings is something that should – and does – unnerve us.

CHAPTER 1: 'YOU'RE SUPPOSED TO BE DOING YOUR HOMEWORK'

There is a concept called liminality. A liminal zone or area is the borderland where everything changes: not as neat and sharp a partition as a straightforward dividing line, but a slightly fuzzier transitional layer, like No Man's Land. It may be between one place and another, past and present, the real and the unreal, light and dark, childhood and adulthood, the living and the dead, this world and another. In **Sapphire & Steel** it's all of them, and this is front-loaded into its first serial, before being reinforced and depicted more obviously in its second.

It's also, appropriately for **Sapphire & Steel**, a good descriptor for that divide between children's TV and mainstream TV, which is hardly surprising since we normally call the division between child and adult 'puberty,' the most liminal – if mythology, folklore and psychology are to be believed (biology is self-evident) – of life's stages. The rites of passage at puberty, whatever they may be in a particular society, are a key element of ritual, and are reflected in our myths and in our cultures. Lack of such rites in some form produces an imbalance in the individual psyche, in the body social, which has to be addressed in some manner. Psychologists and students of myth have seen fantasy, myth and fiction occupying these roles[7].

Rob, the young boy who serves as the audience viewpoint character in *Assignment One*, is the recipient of the line 'You're supposed to be doing your homework,' which was and is, a common refrain in the households in which the series was viewed. In those days,

---

[7] Selected works that do this include Joseph Campbell, *The Hero with a Thousand Faces* (1949); Mircea Eliade, *Rites and Symbols of Initianion,* transl. Willard R Trask (1998); William Bascomb, 'The Myth-Ritual Theory', in *The Journal of American Folklore*, Vol. 70, #276 (1957).

children's TV was ring-fenced in particular time slots, and had specific aims, whether it be as a background to homework, a break from it, or a reward for it.

From the opening of the first episode, this line symbolises an intent to make a link between the child characters and the audience at home; obviously a common theme in children's TV drama such as *Assignment One*. *Assignment Two*, on the other hand, is not children's drama; the series has reached adulthood already.

Sapphire & Steel's puberty, so to speak, occurred in reality during the writing and filming stage, when what had been commissioned as a children's fantasy drama had been rescheduled to a later 'family drama' slot[8] due to *Assignment One* being deemed a bit too spooky and scary, but also too good to scrap. Once ATV had made that change, the show's creators were freed to go further than the strictures of the Children's Drama department might be comfortable with.

Nowadays audiences are used to shows targeting a range of different audiences by age: toddlers, children, pre-teens, late-teens, tweens, young adults, new adults... There are not just programmes but whole channels, aimed squarely at as many demographics as can be imagined, just as there are in books (of which even the term 'Young Adult' for the crossover between fiction and children's fiction only dates from 1962[9]).

In the 1970s, however, things were very different in terms of drama on British TV. There was Drama, there was Educational Broadcasting (TV for Schools), and there was Children's Drama. Age suitabilities were guided by the various watersheds, mainly the 9pm one, seen as the main for-adults borderline.

---

[8] Cornell, Paul, Day, Martin and Keith Topping, *The Guinness Book of Classic British TV*, p.350.
[9] Dunning, Stephen, 'Criticism and the "Young Adult Novel"' (1962).

Children's TV services in Britain began on the BBC in 1946 with **For the Children**, an hour-long live broadcast on Sunday afternoons, for an intended audience of toddlers through to primary-age pupils.

From there, the BBC began to lead the field in magazine and documentary programming for junior viewers. The Arts predictably got a junior strand, but there were also sports programmes, and current affairs shows, and quiz shows. In these fields, ITV somewhat lagged behind, but still managed to produce **Magpie** (1968-1980) as an equivalent to **Blue Peter**, and science and history programming like **How!** (1966-1981).

On the children's drama front, the BBC's larger nationwide budget and reputation allowed it to pull ahead of ITV in terms of quality output, although ratings remained competitive throughout. While the BBC tended to focus on adaptations of books, ITV focused on original screen ideas. This meant that BBC children's drama tended to look better and gain more favourable press, but ITV children's drama tended to be more adventurous and action-oriented. ITV shows also often had have longer seasons, because they were specially developed rather than drawn from a pre-existing work of a relatively trim word-count.

Assignment One's setting of an old solid house, and the historical angle brought by the Roundheads and plague victims, combine with the short serial format of a six-episode single story to give the show more of a BBC children's drama feel. **Sapphire & Steel** was taking the BBC on in its strongest game rather than the traditional ITV adventure format.

That was a bold and confident move, especially since the show would be entirely studio-bound and shot on video, eschewing the location filming enjoyed by other ITV serials like **Timeslip** (1970) or **Children of The Stones** (1977), both of which featured mind-bending time elements, or ITV's own book adaptations, such as **The Owl Service** (1969).

The closest thing to a Young Adult drama demographic was so-called 'Family Drama' in an evening slot, but this was not a separate department at any of the TV stations. Family drama was simply drama produced by the Drama departments, which happened to be considered not too strong for any audience member likely to be watching. (It was expected that families would watch together over dinner.)

This was a somewhat undefined transitional middle-ground; a liminal slot, in which the first two **Sapphire & Steel** stories – which had been recorded together in one fourteen-episode block – transitioned from childhood to adulthood, both on set and in front of the viewers' eyes.

Assignment One is, as stated previously, a Children's serial. This is clear in many ways, not least the fact that the audience identification figures are both children; Rob, who looks to be around twelve or fourteen, and his younger sister Helen. The two main characters are a male and female pairing in loco parentis, and Lead is a jovial giant, who encourages the two kids to sing, and probably wouldn't be out of place hosting a Saturday morning show. There are no deaths in the serial, and there's even a clear-cut happy ending.

Assignment Two, however, is a complete reversal. Such audience identification characters as there are comprise of an older man and a ghostly soldier. The closest thing to a children's audience-identification is Sapphire acting as the proxy voice for a young teacher on whom the soldier had a crush at school nearly seventy years earlier. Multiple deaths are re-enacted, jollity is sparse, and the ending is far from a happy one.

What we see in these fourteen episodes is, therefore, a TV drama cross a threshold between two areas of target demographic, passing through the liminal zone of the 'family drama' timeslot. This is very different than the norm, where a series would be commissioned as an adult drama suitable for the 'family drama' timeslot, rather than changing in the middle of the first production block's writing.

On screen, Rob himself also seems to be on the cusp of puberty. Again, this is a transformational border between childhood and adulthood, and simple to recognise as a biological mechanism. It's also, appropriately enough for a drama focusing on the supernatural effects of time going wrong, and which contains ghosts and (in *Assignment Two*) spiritualistic séances with Sapphire acting as a medium[10] — also something that comes to the fore in many Fortean tales of ghosts and poltergeists. Such reports throughout the 20th Century often focused on members of the affected family who had hit reached puberty and in the few years after. The Enfield Poltergeist, investigated by Maurice Grosse between 1977 and 1979 (and featured in national and local news programmes during that time), is the seminal British example[11]. Another famous case includes the Rosenheim Poltergeist in 1967[12]. Pretty much every issue of *Fortean Times* has an example. Rob is just the right age.

Returning to the power of names, Sapphire and Steel themselves also understand that names have meaning and words have power. Steel in particular is very forceful and insistent about wanting to know the name of the soldier ghost in *Assignment Two*. He asks the ghost directly, with fake jollity, and then later bullies both Sapphire

---

[10] Another change from the documentation for the commissioning of *Assignment One* as a children's series accepting a requirement that any apparently supernatural activity has a (pseudo)scientific explanation. And they don't try very hard in that story either, as the change had happened before filming. (Network DVD viewing guide)
[11] Playfair, Guy Lyon, *This House Is Haunted*, (1980) itself adapted into a British serial, *The Enfield Haunting* by Sky in 2015.
[12] **Arthur C Clarke's World of Strange Powers** (1985) episode 2, *Things That Go Bump in The Night*.

herself, the girl she channels, and Tully, with increasingly angry demands to know the soldier's name. Perhaps he merely needs a name to look up in some type of records, but his anger suggests something more. More tellingly, the fact that the Darkness and Pearce appear to be riled by this focus on the name, and that the impromptu séance goes more easily when Tully specifies that he does *not* want the name, tell us that there is something deeper going on.

It may also be worth noting that Pearce is one letter out from Peace, and a homonym for pierce, considering what we discover about his death, shot and pierced by barbed wire after peace had been declared. His name definitely has a meaning, and his reluctance to have it divulged suggests it may have some power over him. Or at least that he worries that it might.

The power of words is doubly true when it comes to their influence on young minds, whether in the form of speech, song, or print. In the modern world, texts in some form make up a huge amount of what children learn. Whether this be in the form of textbooks, stories, or text messages on their phones. The words they speak and hear shape their development, and also show it to others.

With this in mind, it's both good and bad to see that Rob and Helen enjoy books and reading, and that their (mostly unseen) parents seem to encourage them in this. Certainly Time, the mysterious enemy trying to break into their house, also encourages them, perhaps understanding the power of words.

Words can have power in different ways than the straightforward communication between individuals. They may not literally fly around the room like the pages of Helen's book of nursery rhymes in *Assignment One*, but they can get into the head and the mind almost against our will – as does 'Goosey Goosey Gander' to Rob, when he finds himself forced to say it aloud in order to summon the Roundheads that almost execute Sapphire.

On one level this summoning shows a sympathy between words and their external effects: the repeated words 'up stairs and down stairs' call the ghostly Roundheads into being on their way upstairs in the house. They are used by the Time Fragments to associate with an effect, and propagate on their own, beyond Rob's reading of the rhyme: once Rob has said the words, other unknown voices take over – perhaps the words making themselves audible in some fashion – a strange process to both characters and audience.

It's a less strange process to us, with the benefit of hindsight. A new cultural paradigm was on the cusp of recognition in the year in which *Assignment One* was produced, but which is now so common we don't give it any more thought than when we share an amusingly-captioned picture of a cat on the internet. We might well call It a *meme*, a discrete unit of story, which functions by replicating discrete cultural elements to which we are particularly susceptible.

A meme functions, according to Susan Blackmore and Richard Dawkins, the original developers of the idea, much in the manner of a virus replicating cells in a new host[13].

This self-replicating 'virus' is an idea, or an image, or a form of culturally-conditioned behaviour, which enters the brain and replicates itself either by retelling the story, by an imitation of behaviour or in a speech pattern, to an audience who will then pass it on it to others. The meme changes subtly in each transmission according to host, but its basic makeup remains the same.

It can be uncomfortable territory to think about; the idea that memes exist independently of us may be meme theory itself acting as a meme and using subtext as its vector, by showing us its persistence. Memes, as folklore epistemologist Dan Sperber tells

---

[13] Dawkins, Richard, *The Selfish Gene* (1976); Blackmore, Susan, *The Meme Machine* (1999).

us[14], can be anything: they can be images or cultural constructs, catchphrases, stories, beliefs, even the misquotes that everyone is sure are correct, but aren't[15].

Returning to that book of nursery rhymes, in *Assignment One* we see that it acts independently, choosing which rhymes are to be read and when, and also escaping in the kitchen and – once kick-started by Rob and Helen in different scenes – reading itself out loud. It is being used by Time, the villain of the piece, and its modus operandi is to repeat and repeat again words and phrases, weaselling their way into the child's brain until they control it, forcing further repetition by the character. That driving out of every other imperative from the character is an imaginative dramatic interpretation of the action of memes.

Rather than the regular action of memes, in which concepts and ideas survive and spread by conforming to a form of natural selection, the sort of possession and control we see attempted by the antagonists in *Assignment One* – and to some degree by the Darkness when it possesses Sapphire in *Assignment Two* – is a less natural form of spread that we more usually see in invasive species, which so often lead to the diminishment or destruction of the native ones[16]. Anyone who has been earwormed by a catchy song in the background knows exactly how this feels.

Professor Jack Zipes, radical theorist of folk tales and Grimm expert who translated the *Tales* for a new 2014 edition, once described the Grimms' tales as 'contagious'[17]. This brings us right back to the idea

---

[14] Sperber, Dan, *Explaining Culture, A Naturalistic Approach*, (1996)
[15] Examples being 'Play it again, Sam' from *Casablanca* (1942) or 'Luke, I am your Father' from *Star Wars: The Empire Strikes Back* (1980)
[16] As grey squirrels have largely driven out red squirrels in the UK.
[17] Zipes, Jack, *The Brothers Grimm: From Enchanted Forests to the Modern World* (2002), p.16.

of stories as memes, spreading themselves virally into children's minds for the past couple of centuries.

There is one cultural aphorism we can't get away from however and it very much contributes to the lasting appeal of *Assignment One*: safe at home in front of the TV, children love being scared. That's the whole appeal of campfire ghost stories, and the like.

A flying book of fairy tales, filled with potential memes, acts as both a scare to children and a hook to adults, as well as a cunning subtext as to the methodology of this highly innovative and multi-layered serial. The book acting as a vector for an invasive meme, however, isn't quite the same as, say, being eaten by a bear. The threat of devourment is one of humanity's oldest fears, burned deep in the mammalian hindbrain from the days when our earliest ancestors were prey for larger creatures.

In the traditional tales, bones are ground to make bread, witches cook children in their stoves, hungry ogres and giants lurk at the tops of beanstalks, but these things are too mundane for this series. Here the devourment is by lights, and dark, and sometimes it is the mind rather than the body being consumed and digested by forces more powerful and inexorable than mere teeth and claws and fur.

While there's a biological impetus to this fear, there are other elements of the human psyche and our living conditions that may be manifested in the fear of devourment, and this opening fourteen-episode block delves more deeply into those than it does into the simplistic hunter-prey relationship of other properties. Folklorist Marina Warner has suggested[18] that 'Much of this lurid cannibalistic material acts as metaphorical disguise for issues of authority... the changing character of such monstrous or diabolical beings as infanticides reveals ideas about authority in the family

---

[18] Warner, Marina, *No Go the Bogeyman* (1998), p.10.

and beyond it; fatherhood, its limits, and its obligations are called into question above all.'

Note that Rob's clearly autocratic father is absent until he arrives to take Rob to the cellar in the penultimate episode of *Assignment One*, and the wide-eyed mother is, at the moment she turns to Rob, an agent of Time, which seeks to 'break in and take things' in exactly the same way the bogeyman as nursery demon steals children. It's an 'enemy Other' in the child's own time and place, which in this case has swallowed up Rob's parents and seeks to take his sister.

The location in which it attempts this is another liminal area: the oldest part of the house, where past and present meet. Here 1979 and 1736 are two separate worlds, sharing the cellar, which is the transitional point between them. This contrasts with the serial's other pair of zones on either side of a transformational border, which are the real world and the representation of it inside a painting. It's not made clear whether the location in the painting is a previous iteration of part of the house, but, given that so much of the focus on the source of the antagonistic power is on Time, this might be a reasonable supposition.

In *Assignment Two*, the Darkness, which is potentially related to Time in some manner, as it can utilise and affect time, swallows rooms, objects, hours, and, indeed, people. The astute will also notice the immediate connection between strangers who arrive in the night and impose authority and Steel, whose first act is to subsume the authority of the local policeman who has been called to deal with Rob's parents' disappearance. Soon after that he similarly subsumes Rob's father's private space, using his study, and manhandling his precious clock collection. Much of the ambivalence – and fascination – around Steel in the first serial derives potentially from such nursery archetypes of the Other, of which Warner's bogeyman is a subspecies.

Ambivalence with regard to authority exists in both Sapphire and Steel from the outset of the series. Though most of the 'bad guys' in the series are either neutral or male, a fraction of doubt remains around the feminine and even around Sapphire, establishing the tension which will exist throughout the series, thanks to an introduction for both viewpoint characters, and their target audience, to an adult world where not everything is as it seems, a threshold crossed from certainty into uncertainty which cannot be crossed back.

That said, we should mention that the only character to be genuinely 'devoured' body and soul, is an adult, Tully the ghost hunter. Is that reassuring? Less so to adults than to children, who have an unfailing sense of the macabre and an understandable pleasure at the inversion of the adults 'getting got' instead of them.

Where Rob's parents appear as evil versions of themselves in the final episode of *Assignment One*, the unease is also generated by another familiar – and feared – figure of folklore. The Doppelgänger (or 'Fetch' to give it its old name) has its own literary and cultural history as an epitome of the familiar gone bad. Folkloric beliefs in many parts of Britain and Scandinavia hold that to see a person's double is a harbinger of death[19].

What we – perhaps surprisingly – don't see in **Sapphire & Steel** is an anthropomorphisation of Time as the antagonist. We see the effects that Time's anger and hunger wreak upon the characters and settings; we see the 'refractions' it uses as tools in *Assignment One*, along with the mysterious patches of light, and we see the Darkness and the more sentient ghosts that it exploits and uses – and feeds upon – in *Assignment Two*. The series as a whole manages to avoid doing that obvious and simple thing; it acknowledges the comparison in its own ways, reflecting our relationships with that particular predator more subtly. Most

---

[19] https://www.britannica.com/art/doppelganger

impressively, it does this in different ways in these two stories, without feeling inconsistent, but instead by building upon the memes and imagery – and at the same time delving more deeply into them.

It's a near-universal human tradition to characterise Time as an implacable, devouring force. This concept is hardwired into our mythologies in an attempt to placate our sense of mortality, and has, largely, not yet been replaced in our everyday perceptions, or our language, by science. We still speak of time pressing upon us, running out, running short, and catching up with us; we still put our own physical forms of predator and prey onto a more conceptual reality of which we are an infinitesimal part.

Time and its denizens in **Sapphire & Steel** seem reminiscent of themes in the Kabbalistic legend of the universe that God got wrong. It's one of those myths which is designed to make sense of the strange and apparently unknowable nature of the world and its place. In the myth, the Demiurge tries to build a universe, while Lilith, Queen of Demons, complains over his shoulder that he's got it wrong. (You may note that Sapphire has to take this tack with Steel on occasion, notably for the first time in *Assignment Two*). He doesn't listen, and the universe ends up abandoned with all the demons – the sheddim, or Shadows – the empty shells of life in it, predictably with Lilith in charge, but still connected to our own universe. It's a myth that works very well with today's physics, where the Universe is thought to be one of many universal bubbles in a multiversal sea.

Of course, it also fits with that tension between our heroes in *Assignment Two*: Steel doesn't listen to Sapphire's advice, presses on with his assumptions about the nature of the threat, and ultimately the increasing number of shadows in the railway station take form as more resentful ghosts, ending up with the destruction of Tully – though it doesn't leave Sapphire in charge of the station, let alone the universe.

There's also a hint of W.H. Auden's very folky, but also uncanny, poem 'As I Walked Out One Evening':

The glacier knocks in the cupboard, the desert yawns in the bed, and the crack in the teacup opens a lane to the Land of the Dead[20].

Human experience and a lot of human literature has been about coming to terms with what Auden describes here: aging and mortality. Chiefly, we try to come to terms with things by giving them a human face, even if by so doing we also ascribe to them the nastier human instincts to do with death.

Chronos, Time, according to the Greeks, was the Titan – a demigod – who devoured his own children. He also ages and dies, and is shown as a bent old man with a scythe, just as in the medieval depictions of Father Time, close cousin to Death, who carries the same implement. Time here is regulated in a natural process with the acquiescence and blessing of the Almighty, as 'to all things there is a time,' as Tully would reassure us.

The issue at the heart of *Assignment Two* in particular – and the series as a whole, when mixing things from different times causes breaches that invite Time and its minions to rampage into human chronology – is that the difference between a person or thing's perceived or intended time, and their actual time is a source of danger, of threat, and of resentment not just from the person, but from Time. In the first serial it's hunger and want that is the commonality shared between humanity and time, while in the second it is anger and resentment that we share.

---

[20] Auden, W.H., *'As I Walked Out One Evening'*.

What sort of face can you put on Time? Usually it is death, but what about time beyond that, or time that is deathless emotion? What and who teaches us when traditional mythology and its initiators fails? Are we absolutely guaranteed that courage - and knowledge - will result in a happy end? What if we just get eaten up anyway? What if the nursery rhymes we all grew up with are really an ingress for Time the devourer, a power constantly seeking to infiltrate? What happens when all of society's cultural, magical, and religious defences against the Darkness break down, and the hungry dead come through demanding retribution?

In the western world we tend to think of Time as a very old man, replaced every New Year with a baby. Here in *Assignment One*, however, Time is described by Sapphire as a corridor, through which things – its agents – can break into our world; in later episodes Time itself is described as breaking through. This is somewhat inconsistent, but what is more consistent is that Time in the series abducts people, and it's telling that *Assignment One* has it threatening two children. Old Father Time, in this serial, is looking to possess and subsume, or potentially kill, his replacement. When Rob and Helen's parents are the images used by Time, the implication is more chilling still, as it is an inversion of the expected progress of human chronology and mortality.

CHAPTER 2: 'DON'T YOU KNOW YOUR HISTORY?' 'I KNOW MINE, YES.'

The question is asked of Steel by Rob, in *Assignment One*, when Steel doesn't know that Cromwell's Roundheads searched houses for people who didn't pray. Steel's answer is a nice touch to imply that he isn't from the same place as Rob. He could be a foreigner (often suspicion.us enough in 20th Century English fiction), but the implication that he is even more different, more Other – and *Alien* is merely Latin for *Other* – is already there.

Does Steel actually *know* his history, rather than just claim to, any more than anyone else *knows* theirs? We do hear the faux voice meant to be Rob's mother remind her son that she taught him about history earlier too. Does Rob know his history? Well, he remembers what he's been taught, but that isn't necessarily a 'yes', especially if the one who taught him didn't know hers.

There's a problem with history. There's an old joke that says 'history isn't what it used to be,' and this often gets used for a tag line or a cheap gag in time travel fiction and media. Thankfully **Sapphire & Steel** avoids that one, but in many ways it's a truism. One retelling on, history is never what it used to be, and there are reasons for that.

History is written by the victors, or so goes the familiar cliché. And that's true, as far as it goes, but very often it's edited, printed, published, retold, and plagiarised into fiction. Those yet to fight their battles, those in search of easy stolen valour, and so forth. And those who would build upon mere history and mere victors. Those who would rather cut history down to story, and then carry it over to myth.

Napoleon Bonaparte used a different turn of phrase; history is a set of lies upon which we all agree, and this phrasing is more true, because people do lie, but they also like to seem agreeable. Equally, lies are more useful, in practical terms, because they can be modified, customised, and developed upon.

History tends, once it's safely out of living memory, to become mythologised to some degree or other. It does so more immediately too, but the degree of epic myth generally increases with time. Convenience is one reason why history becomes myth; probably the most common reason of all, rather than being a matter of 'out of sight, out of mind' by reason of distance: What's easier to remember, what's catchy (like a nursery rhyme) sticks.

So, what history did Rob, or his mother, not know?

MOTHER

And a lot of nursery rhymes are a part of history, I've always taught you that, haven't I, Rob?

ROB
I'm too old to say nursery rhymes!'

MOTHER
Very well, then. Let's call it history!

We may not all know that 'Goosey Goosey Gander' dates from the English Civil War, but we all know that 'Ring A Ring O Roses' is about the Plague, with the line 'A-tish-shoo, a-tish-shoo, we all fall down' being a disturbingly pointed reference to the speed with which the Black Death, bubonic plague, killed its victims.

Despite the very convincing repetition of their origins in the serial, and a reliance on it to fuel the plot, the esoteric and sinister nursery rhymes of *Assignment One* don't date from those events at all. As Iona and Peter Opie, authors of *The Singing Game*, the seminal work on children's playground rhymes, confirm, there is absolutely no basis for either rhyme's commonly-believed origin. 'Ring A Ring O Roses' cannot be traced back in any recorded form beyond the late 18th century, and is probably a circle dance, and may be partly related to 'European witch dances,' or at least dances thought to be performed by witches, because the dancers danced back to back, an inversion of normality which means people probably just also mythologised the witches into the frame. Otherwise the main part of its origins are earlier dances for children at weddings (the falling down part was originally meant for one child in each turn of the song to reveal what gift they had brought, like musical chairs without a chair crossed with pass the parcel.) The associations with the plague are completely spurious, as the Opies detail[21].

Similarly, 'Goosey Goosey Gander' is only half to do with Cromwell's New Model Army looking for un-pious people in the Puritan age. 'Goose' was 18th Century slang for a lady practitioner of the oldest profession, which is why people keep wandering upstairs and downstairs at her lodgings[22]. That's the first half of the rhyme. The second half, about finding an old man up there and throwing him down the stairs, was derived from an earlier rhyme about craneflies and does relate to the fate of torturing fugitives found in Priest-holes. These two separate four-line rhymes were merged around the turn of the 19th Century[23].

As the Opies point out, most apparently nonsense rhymes for children, like 'Yankee Doodle Dandy' or 'Georgie Porgie', in fact have a saucy or a politically satirical origin, and often both. But such slang and such political satires are things of limited lifespan; mortal, their meanings fade and die when politics move and colloquialisms go out of fashion. Rebellious youth, and naughty children, would have sung these rhymes when they were current, but by the time their meanings have faded and adults only hear nonsense words,

---

[21] See the *Oxford Book of Nursery Rhymes* (1951), in which the full original texts of all the rhymes in *Assignment One* can be found.
[22] Cocker, Mark and Richard Mabey, *Birds Britannica* (2005)
[23] Iona and Peter Opie, *The Oxford Dictionary of Nursery Rhymes*.

they are thought of as children's songs, and are taught as that thereafter.

Of course, *Assignment One* so added to the perception of the plague rhyme origin that it's sometimes quoted as evidence much in the way that popular folklore now only has werewolves transforming at full moon[24] and being killed by silver bullets, thanks to Curt Siodmak's rhyme in 1941's *The Wolf Man*.

But if the rhymes don't have this deep connection, if it's all made up, why do they have such an effect when they are used here? The answer lies in a device common to religion, magic, and magicians and, for that matter used by political demagogues like Hitler – repetition. Repetition has a tendency to reinforce our beliefs, for good or ill.

That's how it's used for everything from religious litanies to political slogans, and why advertising copywriters are paid to dream up repeatable phrases. Repetition can even, so the theory goes, send us in to a different level of consciousness. That's the basis behind repeating the *jewel in the lotus* (*om mane padme hum*) in meditation. The liminal effect, carrying you across the transition to the altered state of consciousness, lies in repeating the rhyme, sometimes repeating it backwards[25] and singling out occasional individual words for the same treatment.

---

[24] In various folklores from around the world, most werewolves became so by the use of potions, bargains with the devil, talismanic objects, and so on. Not by being bitten by another werewolf – in the folklore there wouldn't be enough left of you to become a new werewolf. Once the film came out, with its opening rhyme, all those things appear to have been forgotten, and being bitten by a werewolf became the default way to get the curse, in the public consciousness. It's also from here that lycanthropy became largely an effect of the full moon rather than a choice of will.

[25] Another favourite trick of ritual magic, somewhat ridiculed by the

Reinforced here with Cyril Ornadel's minimalist music in the minor key, voice modulations to induce anxiety and slight distorting sound effects, mainly layering the voices and adding echo and a wind-like whisper, they are effective in creating that eerie feeling because they have touched on some deeper chord.

The spoken word, not even needing to rhyme or be sung (though the repetition in notes or rhyming couplets adds a flow to relax the speaker and audience into their desired state of consciousness), is the oldest form of both mythology and history, long before anyone tried to separate those two things. Go back far enough, and all tales were oral tales; songs, poems, and campfire stories. Some were intended to pass along knowledge or history, others to inform politically and practically, and of course, we can presume some simply to entertain.

History also works upon us. We are the sums of our memories, our laws are judged by precedent, our politics by age-old fears, desires, and drives. The present, of any era, wants to make its mark because it knows that it will one day be history. It knows it is mortal; nobody lives forever, but neither does any state, any moment, any nation, any movement. Time is our ally and our enemy, helping us along only because it leads us to where it wants us.

We know our history, and the age of our planet, so the bogeyman gets banished, with successive ages of enlightenment from way back when and into other dimensions, vouchsafed us by quantum physics. That leaves carte blanche for writers hiding anything in a dimensional fold, including hell, or a sentient and hostile Time.

What's interesting is that, as with the nursery rhymes, the relationship between history and mythology goes both ways; as

---

Master's use of 'Mary Had A Little Lamb' – an American poem by Sarah Josepha Hale, dating from 1830, in case you're wondering – in the **Doctor Who** story *The Dæmons* (1971).

well as history becoming mythologised, so mythology can become historicised. In this, Rob's mother – real and ersatz versions – is correct. In *Assignment One* Time uses these mythologies to connect to history, and to summon assistants from history due to the connection between the two. Roundheads and plague victims were real history, summoned to the house by the repetition of myths in the form of rhyming couplets. It's also interesting that the house itself post-dates both the last great plague and the era of Roundheads, the first stone having been laid in 1736, according to Rob in the cellar in episode six. It's worth noting that, like the house, 'Goosey Goosey Gander' in its eight-line form also dates to the eighteenth Century.

Mythology becomes history when we deconstruct it, examine it, and use it as a trail of breadcrumbs to follow in search of true histories, but it also becomes history itself as it ages. Stories and songs change over time and are reinterpreted. The histories of the different versions myths and stories and songs themselves in different eras and locations become history. This isn't just true of nursery rhymes, where ammunition for Time's attack on the house of *Assignment One* is concerned, but would also be available to it in other forms of literature that the likes of Rob and Helen would know.

Like the children tuning in to watch at home, Rob and Helen, as readers who clearly enjoy their rhymes and tales, probably knew their Grimm's fairytales. And if they adhered to Ogden Nash's belief mentioned earlier, they will have loved those tales of devourment, children lost in woods, and brutal punishments doled out to those who were naughty. So, undoubtedly, would Time, as the Grimms, again, can be viewed as turning mythology into history.

The heroes in the Grimms' tales are out and out rebels, and independence of thought and bravely facing dangers are good yet potentially dangerous traits. This fits Rob quite well, as we'll see, though the Grimms' tales are more violent, yet far less terrifying, in concept than **Sapphire & Steel**.

That Rob and Helen, like every child watching Sapphire and Steel's first outing, had probably already been vicariously exposed via the safe pages of a book to beatings, whippings, dismemberment, bloody revenge, creatures that snatch children in the night, and a host of other horrors has a great bearing on why scenes such as Sapphire's ravaged face didn't get the show taken off air. They legitimised horrific tales of a certain sort as suitable for children.

One of the greatest myths about the Grimms' tales is that they were all written for children. They weren't. Like Giovanni Francesco Straparola's *The Facetious Nights of Straparola*, a two-volume collection of 75 fairy-tales from 1550, they had been published for an adult audience.

Of course, they weren't. The Grimms were librarians, looking to track the history of these stories and how they developed in the areas they came from, and why. 'It's nice that people think that,' Jacob Grimm commented about the idea of the tales as being meant for children in a letter of 1812, 'but they weren't.'[26] The tales were anthologised and published for adults at a specific historical point in time, and under specific cultural conditions, some of which (paradigm shifts, economic upheavals, questions of national identity that would eventually lead to the formation of a single Germany, class strictures, and occupation by foreign military forces) were very relevant when **Sapphire & Steel** was made. In 1980, Germany was still split into East and West, with several European countries garrisoned by Soviet forces. They were Geiger counters of the Zeitgeist, and anything that references them tends to have the same quality, especially when watched by adults.

---

[26] Quoted in Zipes, *Brothers Grimm*.

They also, contrary to popular belief, weren't just folktales for the sake of being entertaining folktales; they had a subtext, and there were reasons why these tales had survived being passed down through time. Some were as much literary fiction written in and of their age, however much they purported to come from a truer, earlier, source or a more native, nationally inspired one than those of their contemporaries. Others, told orally of course, were intended to guide behaviour: if your country is occupied by a foreign army, there are good reasons for not, say, creeping around the woods. The collecting of the tales was constructed with particular ends in mind, not least the encoding of social and political themes to work around the censorship of a Germany occupied by Napoleon. (At least in the first two editions of the Grimms, after which Wilhelm Grimm started to edit them into forms more attractive to middle-class urban parents who wanted to read them to children simply as pleasant entertainment.)

Transformative literature has always been a locus for rebellion, a place where the ignored, the dispossessed, and the forgotten have found a voice; a place to be raucous and bawdy, and out of order. The location changes with each generation, as do the tricks they employ to get noticed, to subvert and bend the rules culturally and stylistically, to win out against attempts at censorship and authority.

The Grimms' tales have something of a split personality – snapped up by educators in the latter 19th century, the later editions of the tales were adapted and often bowdlerised to promote conformity and to strengthen the role of authority figures and reinforce contemporary gender roles in ways absent from the originals. The beloved Frog Prince, for example, isn't kissed by his princess in the original version; he's hurled violently against the wall in disgust, ejected from her bed with such force 'that all his bones break.'. This usurping of male violence makes him transform into the prince, and later editors and educators took that out.

Although rebels in their own right – Jacob admitted in his letters that he longed to escape his mundane job, and just walk into the forests he referenced in his tales and keep going[27] – the Brothers, unlike some of their more aristocratic writer-cousins, were firmly embedded in the world of bourgeois middle class aspirations[28]; a world that transfers over to the milieu in which we meet Rob and Helen in *Assignment One*.

Theirs is a very middle class, ordered childhood. There is homework (which Rob *should* be doing), stories at bedtime, a kitchen as centrepiece of familiar interaction and socialising, a study sacred to the patriarch, which must not be entered, and clocks ticking everywhere. Ticking away the beat of regimented life. The breaking of precisely this order constitutes the beginning of the story.

The Grimms, then, are a heady inheritance, and we should not be surprised, with their influence on board, even subtextually, if traditional literature does try to escape its confines, in this show's case quite literally.

A less obvious connection between the Grimms' collecting of folk tales and *Assignment One* is that they actually got the stories by having groups of women come to their house specifically to retell the tales they had grown up with (William in fact married one of them), making Rob's mother's persuasion of him by comparing them to history, along with her reading to Helen, a quite accurate reflection of how the brothers worked. In leading with mythology, she resonates history, however subconsciously.

---

[27] Ibid.

[28] The sons of a lawyer, their family faced financial difficulty after his death. Fortunately, his sister was able to secure the boys an education at the University of Marburg, after which they became librarians.

That uneasy border between rebellion and authority, particularly in the figures of Rob and his absent, abducted, father, is another reason why this series offers both compelling viewing and innovation. In a traditionally middle-class reality, outside of TV, rebellious youth is generally seen as something to be discouraged, demonised, and blamed for society's ills, yet in fiction the opposite is the case.

In both 20th Century children's literature and subsequently TV and film, it's much more often the case that adult authority figures on the 'good' side of things are either ineffectual or rendered absent by circumstances, so that it's left to the youth of the day to disobey — but in the right way, which usually leads to putting themselves in danger, but also solving the problem at hand.

In Rob this is exactly what is shown here, children entering and dealing with an adult world of the Other, of threats and disruptions to their established world view. It's the world of every fairytale in which a deemed stupid third son, or a princess defying gender stereotypes, sets off to find themselves on a quest or fish a golden ball from a well, in prime time viewing. This feeds back directly into those eerie eyes that permeate the series, and the tropes of bogeyman, child snatcher, and villain who are not real people (as in the Grimms') but shapeless devouring darkness capable of stealing people into paintings or making them relive the deaths of others from long ago.

CHAPTER 3: 'LOOKING THROUGH FROSTED GLASS'

The biggest mythologisation, especially in genre fiction, is probably Joseph Campbell's Monomyth, or the Hero's Journey. This theory, originally mooted in 1949 in Campbell's book *The Hero with a Thousand Faces*, still holds sway today over much of the culture industry. Campbell's Monomyth, an underlying structure identified in folklore, myth, legend, and the hagiography and rituals of world religions – and by association, in those creative works which draw from these sources – concerns a Hero's (though this really means protagonist or audience identification character) separation from the world of the everyday. The Hero will encounter the otherworldly, have adventures, undergo initiation and transformation, and return to the ordinary world bestowed with a boon of knowledge, or a magical object which can effect a transformation. If the pattern sounds familiar it will be in part because this structure, and the subsets Campbell identified of the three-part progression of separation-initiation-return, form the basis of George Lucas's **Star Wars** series.

To this day, screenplays in Hollywood are often assessed against Campbell's benchmark despite the fact that the theory contains significant points of contention to a modern audience. The central identification character is a hero, not a heroine; female figures are confined to the roles of mother, goddess, lover, imitator, and also destroyer. Campbell's patterning across world myth and belief from a Western Christian cultural perspective is additionally extremely problematic in our post-colonial age. Nevertheless, it is the prevailing theory of the appropriate creative approach to the otherworldly in the years in which **Sapphire & Steel** was written. In its context the series and individual episodes can be read in several different ways.

The character Rob in *Assignment One* is ideal for patterning on to this structure, but only partially as the hero. When we first meet him, he is clearly on the threshold of adolescence and yet in other ways is treated by the script as a child. With his parents absent – abducted by Time, or the creatures that break through from it – he is forced to some extent to step into their shoes, primarily as he is the person who knows the most about the house. Thus, he assumes the role of guide.

Helen also undergoes her own journey, having to think less like a child, and discount what she has been taught in school for experiential conclusions. She wants the shard of light to be a younger child, or almost a pet, but has to admit it is an alien thing. Equally she has to abandon both 'what we learned in school' and her book of rhymes and rely on her own experience.

The aspects of separation-initiation-return can be patterned on to Rob – Helen doesn't get the initiation part in her character arc – as, in the course of the story, he becomes more adult, exercises his judgement, learns discernment, and returns to his own world with an understanding of something beyond it. He has learned that not all received opinion is correct, that not all authority can be trusted, and that it is important to be able to trust one's own instincts. These things are all part of growing up.

At the same time P.J. Hammond is saying to the child viewer, 'it's OK to question, to explore, to form an opinion,' without denying that the world can sometimes be a complicated or scary place, and that these things must be done with discretion. Hammond is also saying 'where you have been, so have others,' and implying that the value of adults lies not in their roles as stern implacable figures of authority – guardians of the gate, like Rob's father who won't let him into his study – but also in their experiences of the road on which the adolescent, in crossing the threshold to adulthood, must travel. This is the form, function and intent of the initiation part of the Monomyth structure.

The hero's return in Campbell's Monomyth is, if anything, as dangerous as his adventures. As he crosses back over the threshold, Campbell suggests that the hero may fail, may become trapped in the Otherworld, and may even die. Even if return is effected, he may find that he simply returns to his own life and 'walled in hard work, culture or boredom,'[29] the adventure and its meaning is soon forgotten. Worse, he may entirely fail to return; if this is willingly, fair enough, but there are also those who get trapped[30].

The stages of the monomyth can as easily be patterned on to Steel as well. For him, our world is the Otherworld, of which he seems to have a limited knowledge, while Sapphire is the more knowledgeable guide, who knows its ways. Steel has a tendency to assume more than he knows, and although he may have acted to bring the knowledge of other worlds and their terrors, dangers, and wonders into our world, in the end he doesn't return to his.

Perhaps it is because the suffering of a child is uncomfortable and unacceptable to an audience, that the serial trials, temptations and sufferings of the monomyth hero are patterned on to Sapphire and Steel instead. In illustrating the hero's tribulations, Campbell uses the Biblical motifs of Jonah being swallowed by the whale, and Christ's wanderings in the desert. Devourment is an ongoing theme, and both Sapphire and Steel are swallowed up by the Darkness. Tully the ghost hunter, on the other hand, is thrown out of his complacent world, where he is bolstered by his religion, into an amorphous realm where none of his prayers work. He is the Monomyth's wizard suddenly derived of his spells, a religious man adrift in a world of faithless horrors, and he doesn't come home either, thanks to one of the starkest and most distressing scenes of the whole series. Of the deaths suffered or experienced in

---

[29] Campbell, Joseph, *The Hero with a Thousand Faces*, p.49
[30] This, in fact, will ultimately be the fate of Sapphire and Steel themselves in *Assignment Six*.

Assignment Two, none are particularly easy, nor quick. There is death on barbed wire, slow suffocation, and burning to death. Not to mention whatever the Darkness actually does, hinted at only by a scream.

The difference is, as Steel mentions, that death on a battlefield or in a burning warplane or sunken vessel is, if not expected, at least to be accepted. Tully's death is intended to be unacceptable. It's intended be a torment, a deliberate sacrifice of one innocent for others. Where the deaths of the ghosts were accidental in nature or timing, Tully's is designed to be deliberately cruel, and this is the choice made by the hero of the series. It's a moral inversion of everything the audience would expect from the good guy solving the problem at hand. For a series that a mere eight episodes ago was a children's programme with ultimately good and caring leads who contrive a happy ending, this is a remarkable turnaround, quite unlike anything else on British TV at the time.

If Steel in his initial appearance is a sarcastic and prickly, but ultimately benevolent, rescuer, a father figure, by the end of the second story he is an uncompromising soldier engaged in a brutal war of attrition. Civilians who get in his way are acceptable casualties, and colleagues are put at risk. It's interesting to see how a relationship of personal animosity and hatred of the 'enemy' develops between the mysterious problem solver and the ghosts' spokesman, Private Pearce. This has elements of the squaddie resenting and trying to get one over on an unpopular officer, or a policeman going out of his way not to co-operate with an Internal Affairs officer or FBI agent undertaking his investigation, let alone the relationship of enemies on opposite sides in a war.

Pearce goes out of his way to be insolent to Steel, to flaunt the deal the Darkness has made with him and at one point puts Steel in a position where he effectively 'frags' him, (military parlance for killing off an unpopular superior and blaming it on friendly fire) ensuring he is lured into a trap and snarled on barbed wire. At which point Pearce settles down to smoke next to Steel and, with history's hatred of the present, gloat as Steel experiences to all intents and purposes, very immediately and physically, Pearce's own death. Steel is certainly put through the wringer here, perhaps because, as the male protagonist, he is in some way closer to the airmen, soldiers and submarine engineers whose ghosts gather on the promise of a new life.

Herein lies one of the most disturbing aspects of **Sapphire & Steel**. If these are the otherworldly figures of our traditional myth, our folklore, if they are the elemental archetypes... If these (mostly) benevolent travellers in time, time-menders (as the original script called them), are the authorities sent to deal with intrusion of horrors into our dimension, then how can there by forces in this universe of which they themselves are very, very, afraid? So afraid, in fact, that one of them is willing to inflict the cruellest possible betrayal upon an innocent in order to placate just such a force.

Where does that leave mortals like Rob and Helen and their parents? It leaves them, as W.H. Auden put it, 'lost in a haunted wood, children afraid of the dark, who have never been happy or good.'[31] It leaves them as small beings with the knowledge excised that there are great powers on either side of their safe middle ground. It leaves them in yet another of the series' layers of liminality.

A sense of liminality, of multiple crossings of threshold and 'zones of power', is essential to Campbell's monomyth. Liminality in **Sapphire & Steel** is an artfully constructed tapestry of sound and vision, a kind of masterclass in creating and maintaining uncanny atmosphere and suspending belief. Some of this is based on the

---

[31] Auden, Wystan Hugh, 'September 1, 1939', in *Another Time* (1940)

manipulation of established tropes, while other aspects are sheer magician's trickery and sleight of hand, either in special effects or in human psychology.

This is amply brought out both in *Assignment One*, where the adversary creates zones of safety and danger using the existing frame work of the house's central staircase. The base of the stairs is a zone of relative safety where Rob, Sapphire, Steel and Lead discuss the case and establish baselines. The first landing is an intermediate zone which is at first safe and then later invaded; the mezzanine, three intermediate steps, is where the soldiers appear and has thus crossed over into the realm of danger. Here we will find the picture which lies in wait and traps Sapphire in an older building on the site where 'something terrible happened,' and a room off the bedroom door under which the shard of light hides. Ascending the stairs, we come to the primary zone of invasion and terror, Helen's room, where the corridor of Time has been breached, allowing refractive figures such as leprous beggar to emerge.

Time (or its agents) has, however, made a mistake: it has attempted to take over the house in reverse, from the top down. Staircases as liminality are regularly used in literature, culture and film as a symbol of shifting identities. They are, for example, a typical location for the ghosts of grey, white, or green ladies in English stately homes. Homi K. Bhaba, who has considered them in post-colonial literature notes,

> the hither and thither of the stairwell, the temporal movement that it involves, prevents identities at either end of it from settling into primordial polarities. the very act of going beyond are unknowable, un-representable without a

return to the present, which in repetition becomes disjointed and displaced[32].

This happens a lot in the series: for instance, the stairs up to the bridge between platforms at the haunted railway station are scenes of unearthly meetings. Again, the most dangerous locations are ones which pass between places; landings, staircases, platforms and the rooms of a deserted hotel. Tully sets up his recording equipment on the stairs. In terms of ghost story liminality this is prime real estate. Finally, of course, in *Assignment Four*, Shape is the traditional man upon the stair who wasn't there.

The liminality may be more obvious in some stories than in others, but it is most deeply used, in multiple layers, in *Assignment Two*. All the story's locations form part of the hauntings at some point, and all are clearly divided into safe and unsafe zones, pockets in which time is invaded by the recollections of one or other ghosts, which have the power to draw in an observer. The railway station is a mixture of times (as had been the cellar in the first story); it's a border between life and death, between the light and the Darkness, its footbridge is a simple liminality between the two platforms, but also between the present day and the realm of the Darkness. The landscape of the story too is mined with them. The threshold crossings to these co-existing zones are indicated by changes in clothing, which morphs as the wearer enters the zone and by atmospheric conditions, the traditional 'cold spots' of the ghost hunter.

The independent existence of these potentially deadly zones is reinforced by narrative repetition within them, with a song, a whistled tune, or a snatch of words being the main recurrences. Again, this echoes the stone tape idea of ghosts as recordings, but here there's a big difference: the ghosts are conscious and sentient,

---

[32] Bhabha, Homi K., *The Location of Culture* (1994), p.4.

trapped, doomed to repeat their last moments in closed loops, and mortals (and immortals) can stumble or be lured into the loop. Rescue is only possible from without, as when Steel rescues Sapphire and Tully by bodily carrying each of them out in turn.

Within the series this liminality of structures works to reinforce and underlay the mythic structure and the realm of the uncanny, which intrudes into the everyday, much as it does in traditional ghost stories. There's a reason, after all, why they often contain isolated houses.

The territory between light and dark – the twilight zone, so to speak (and **The Twilight Zone**'s opening narration gives an excellent list of liminal things[33]) – epitomises the liminal. Most of us, to a greater or lesser extent are afraid of the dark. Not the neon-lit dark of cities but the absolute dark in a lonely unlit landscape. We're predisposed to see things in it. Researchers in the area of intersection between human imagination, perception and the esoteric – what Patrick Harpur termed 'daimonic reality'[34] – report experiences with 'patches of moving darkness,' and folklore recounts tales of amorphous and animal-like black shapes such as Black Shuck[35], though unaccompanied by the rustling sounds the Darkness makes when it 'eats' rooms round Sapphire, Tully, and Steel.

From a different angle, Paul Devereux, a researcher into Earth Mysteries, Earthlights[36], and the alleged influence of power lines

---

[33] 'It is the middle ground between light and shadow, between science and superstition, and it lies between the pit of man's fears and the summit of his knowledge.'
[34] Harpur, Patrick, *Daimonic Reality: A Field Guide to the Otherworld* (1994)
[35] The phantom hound viewed as a harbinger of death in East Anglia.
[36] The study of Fortean subjects related to geographical and geological features, such as ancient burial mounds, so-called ley

and the like on the human brain, reports similar moving patches of darkness or mist[37]. Some communal archetype is perhaps at work here. The Darkness in the series preys on our deepest fears: What comes after death? Do the dead harbour grudges? Is there something – not someone – behind the curtains, lurking in the shadows, and in many ways horribly familiar?

Liminality itself is a very Fortean area, between reality and fiction; in the rational, empirical world, and in folklore and mythology, it is an amorphous place of trials, temptations, uncertainties and dangers. Joseph Campbell most often casts it as the 'road of trials', the first part of the hero's journey. Normally the audience is supposed to identify with being in the mortal Everyman's shoes as he or she undertakes the journey. Rob takes this role in *Assignment One*, but from the second story onwards, it is Sapphire and Steel themselves who undertake the journey and find themselves on uncertain ground even by their standards. This is one of the basic and inspired subversions at the heart of this series.

The reason it's a subversion of the norm is because in any other hero's journey, they would be the mysterious supernatural advisors whom the mortal character on the journey would meet, not the ones undergoing trials and disruption to their own established world view, experiencing ordeals, fear and danger.

The beauty and terror of **Sapphire & Steel** in its storytelling is that we are never at ease. Even the adversaries, and their motives, constantly change. They and their stories do that by constantly leading us down the garden path, establishing familiarity, and then moving the goalposts so that we are back in the territory of the unfamiliar, without a roadmap. Time is first said to be a corridor, a

---

lines, and (in the case of Earthlights) aurorae generated by pressures on rock layers with piezo-electric effects.

[37] For instance, *Fortean Times* #366, #367 (2018)

dimension which breaks in to the present as if through thin stretched fabric; then it is somewhere in which unspecified 'things' wait from the end and beginning of eternity. The Darkness has emotion and intent, or it does not, or it uses something which does, depending on the scene, and what Sapphire or Steel's current feelings about it are at that moment.

Or, to put it another way, as much as we adapt ourselves, the shadow, the Other, which this series is masterful at tapping into and putting a face to, is also transformative. The Roundheads who nearly execute Sapphire in *Assignment One*, for example, are first described as merely 'visual refractions' before Rob queries the description.

ROB

Visual refractions?

SAPPHIRE

You'd probably call them... what would he call them?

STEEL

Ghosts.

These ghosts are constrained to repeat the same steps in the same part of the staircase, then break down the same door, again and again.

Such repetition of action is often called a stone tape recording. The theory goes that the chemicals in brick, notably ferrous oxide, work the same way as do ferrous particles on magnetic recording tape, which can record emotional incidents by the electrical activity in the brain rearranging the particles, and then can be replayed by certain circumstances or by the right kind of brain.

One would perhaps expect a recording to degrade over time and use, but this isn't the case with *Assignment One*'s Roundheads: in their second appearance they are more aggressive and threatening, but still unable to manifest in our time. Then suddenly they are fully manifest under Time's control, with both freedom of movement and murderous intent. They may be from the Civil War, but change those uniforms, and their actions of invasion, occupation and murder are, still with us in many places today – and in terms of the religious and political schism they represent, 1979 was still the midst of the Troubles in Northern Ireland, with troops hunting paramilitaries (and vice versa).

Historically those Roundheads would be hunting both Royalists and Catholics, after all. This background of war, tragedy and persecution, and the place of those things in our modern consciousness is one that would be explored from a different angle in *Assignment Two*.

The sense that anything could be out there, and that the slightest move, even an innocent gesture such as the reading of a nursery rhyme, could open us up to a world below, beneath, beyond, or even behind the safe and everyday is fairly explicit in the series. This is, as Douglas Adams would have put it, 'perfectly normal paranoia,' but it's a sense that runs through a lot of our folklore, most of our myth and legend, almost everything in the Western canon we read as children and the vast library of the literature of fantasy.

Both Steel and Sapphire make the existence of this Otherworld and especially of threshold crossings entirely explicit in their operations. However, it should be obvious — especially if we consider Liz and Tully – that the return journey does not always quite work as one might think, and the forces on the other side are not necessarily benign. They are alien and inhuman to a degree well beyond a mortal frame of reference, although they are able to manipulate our humanity. Time in *Assignment One* breaks through in a house –

and, by implied extension, houses – where many different eras are jumbled, old buildings, old foundations, old furniture, old things, old family names, old memories: everything, in fact, that we, as humans, hold on to in our attempts to combat our own mortality. History, by which we define and explain ourselves, and whose objects we cherish, in whose continuity and care we place ourselves, is not our friend in this series.

Of course, **Sapphire & Steel**, is hardly the only British science fiction to reflect or illuminate these uncomfortable perceptions. The **Quatermass** franchise does so in its stark ending, as do the darkest moments of **Doctor Who**.

But, unusually, in **Sapphire & Steel** we encounter the implied question whether what we – as human beings – have done to one another historically is worse than what the Darkness – and even Steel – does to the people they encounter. Neither the Darkness nor Time have a conscience, as we are supposed to have. Steel may well have, yet it is he who makes the cruel decision which condemns Tully.

If anything, that's what connects Steel most strongly to humanity. Not some **Star Trek**-like higher quality of wisdom, but his capability to be arrogantly cruel and vengeful in pursuit of his goals, and the willingness knowingly to cut moral corners when he deems it necessary.

When it comes to time and its denizens in general, **Sapphire & Steel** suggests that humanity has been skating on thin ice for some time. We are perilously close to that dizzying sense of the ground falling away beneath you to reveal what E.T.A. Hoffmann called 'a marvellous world of terror and wonder,'[38] where, according to Joseph Campbell, 'fabulous forces are encountered,' and TS Eliot's

---

[38] Hoffmann, E.T.A, *Tales of Hoffmann*. Author's translation.

'the way, in a dark wood in a bramble, On the edge of a grimpen, where is no secure foothold, And menaced by monsters, fancy lights, Risking enchantment.'[39]

---

[39] Eliot, T.S., 'East Coker'.

CHAPTER 4: 'THEY WERE ALL YOUNG; THE SOLDIER, THE PILOT, THE MEN FROM THE SUBMARINE'

If mankind's favourite occupation has always been war, it's no surprise that it is also one of his favourite subjects – probably, with the possible exception of sex, his favourite subject singular – to read and write about.

Though there are some commonalities in development, each nation has its own kinds of war story, and **Sapphire & Steel**, as a British TV show, is steeped more in the particularly British war genre on which its audience grew up. It is that which it echoes, reflects, undercuts, and counterpoints. The war story, like the ghost story, has a particular resonance to British audiences, and, more so, to British culture and society. This may be partly because the nation is an island one, which has been invaded so many times over the centuries. The two World Wars made an obvious impact, and the Second World War, in particular, has been the central foundation stone of the modern British war story but even before those, there were developments in the genre that soaked into our cultural zeitgeist.

The War story genre as we'd recognise it is really a post-Napoleonic literary invention. Obviously, mankind has made war since one caveman bashed another over the head with a rock, and war has featured in much of his creative art and literature for almost as long, but this literature didn't start off with the sort of novel we expect. To begin with, writing down stories or illustrating scenes and symbols was simply a way of establishing a history, and a cultural memory, by setting in stone who had won what; also it was used to blend mythology with tribal history, to give a basis for the creation and defence of societies in particular areas. This, essentially, is what the Ancient Egyptians did with their paintings and carvings, and then the Homer did for the Greeks, for example.

War was recounted in histories, by the likes of Julius Caesar, to record what had happened. Even the Ancient Greeks, however, added some commentary on how it felt for the combatants, though this wasn't in the narrative prose form we're familiar with in novels today. It was a more metatextual attempt to help audiences understand what their warriors went through (even when it was meant as a declamation against war, as some philosophers and sages did make even then). This kind of historicity continued throughout European history, and also the histories of other civilisations, such as China or Japan. And everywhere, of course, it was mythologised, as history eventually almost always is.

British war novels experienced an evolution particular to the island nation, with post-Napoleonic novels largely falling under the subgenre of Invasion Fiction, in which assorted foreign powers attempted to trample the green and pleasant land underfoot, having crossed the channel in barges.

As you might expect, the First World War produced an unprecedented number of war novels, from all nationalities.

In 1918, however, an English writer named Rebecca West gave us a novel worth mentioning on several counts. *The Return of The Soldier* was the only war novel published by a woman during the Great War; it was the first major novel to focus upon the psychological effects of combatants recovering after they came home from war in what was then called shell-shock, but we'd now call PTSD.

It is of relevance here because we can see the genesis of Private Sam Pearce and his resentment in the suffering of Captain Christopher Baldry and his family.

Other writers would also follow a similar line – most notably Virginia Woolf's *Mrs Dalloway* – and American writers and filmmakers would catch up in the wake of the Vietnam War, but Private Pearce's descent from the novel, even subconsciously or by the memetic transfer of that ancestor through its influence on later works, is difficult to dispute.

In the novel, Captain Baldry is lost in time, at least within his own perceptions, which are related to us through his wife's cousin, the viewpoint character. He actually believes himself to be living 15 years in the past, before the war. He has flashbacks, blending the two different time zones. There's also a psychoanalyst out to cure him of his shell-shock, regardless of whether that's actually the best thing for him, and there's a slight echo of that in Steel's attitude to Pearce in *Assignment Two*. When he is forcibly 'cured,' it is done by means of making him confront not his own death, but that of his infant son, a dozen years earlier, which involves much resentment among the characters, including his current love interest, who isn't his wife.

When he is 'cured' he's actually left with nothing – no wife, no girlfriend, and a dead son – and will have to face all the horrors he endured during the war in addition to that bereavement; a permanent set of nightmares for the rest of his life. The novel wonders whether he was actually better off as he was – the mind had, after all, moved him in time for a good reason – or whether his dignity in knowing the truth needs to win out. It's possible to see some of this in *Assignment Two*, along with viewing the constructed reality in which Captain Baldry lives as a mixture of Tully's view of the nature of the ghost, and the Darkness's promise to Pearce.

Sapphire's more sympathetic view of the ghosts echoes the women in the novel in places, and when she takes on the persona of Pearce's girlfriend, the romantic history recital is reminiscent of the novel's section on Baldry and Kitty's meeting 15 years prior to the main setting. Steel would mostly map onto the psychoanalyst, as would Sapphire in other scenes, while Tully's attitudes reflect that of the narrator, who at least doesn't share his fate, though it is clear at the end of the book that she recognises that she may well have made a mistake. As, of course, did Steel, before correcting it by sacrificing Tully.

Pearce has to face the reality of his youthful death, and that the resumption of his existence is a lie on the part of the Darkness; where Baldry is left with the truth of loveless life of bad memories, Pearce is left with only the truth of his own non-existence and the fact that he's been used and discarded in death as he had been in life. Both characters lose their happy illusions for a painful emptiness.

That Pearce has what we now call PTSD is beyond doubt. If we look at the NHS's own guidelines about PTSD, we find much that matches Pearce in particular – and by extension some of the other ghosts in the serial.

Top of the NHS list of symptoms is re-experiencing the trauma, in the form of flashbacks, with nightmares, troubling imagery, and physical effects like pain, sweating, nausea or trembling. Pearce, of course, certainly has flashbacks, except that, thanks to the power of the Darkness, they can draw other people in and make them experience the flashback, and other troubling imagery and sensations too. He's also jittery when stressed, unsurprisingly.

PTSD sufferers can fall prey to negativity about what happened to them, in particular wondering why it happened to them and if they could have done anything to stop it. They may feel guilt or shame[40]. Once again, Pearce's resentment about what happened to him is the keystone of the plot, and the submarine engineers are heard repeatedly asking why they are trapped, dying, and where they are.

---

[40]   https://www.nhs.uk/conditions/post-traumatic-stress-disorder-ptsd/symptoms/

Trying to avoid being reminded of the trauma, just as Pearce tries to avoid talking to Steel, is another symptom of PTSD. Distraction techniques are common, for example trying to use hobbies to avoid memories; it'd be hard for a ghost to take up gardening, but Pearce still likes to make flowers appear on the platform and talk about what they mean to him. Then there's 'emotional numbing,' the attempt to distance oneself from feeling anything, leading to isolation and withdrawal. A solitary ghost haunting a deserted railway platform, not talking to (mortal) people is about as withdrawn as it's possible to get.

Let's not forget hyperarousal – that is, being anxious and on edge – and both being aware of constantly looking out for threats, and concurrently being angry at being in that state, and so producing irritability and displays of anger. Pearce is very sharp and snappy – vengeful, even – with Steel throughout the serial.

Finally, there's insomnia and difficulty sleeping, whether due to general anxiety and tension, or being awakened by nightmares. Obviously, that's not going to be an issue for an actual ghost like Private Pearce, but still, a ghost walking isn't resting, in peace or otherwise.

Any British viewer old enough to have watched **Sapphire & Steel** on first transmission would have grown up on a diet of Second World War films and similarly themed TV shows. Any Briton over about 40 will know the nostalgic significance of the phrase 'Broadsword calling Danny Boy'[41].

During the Second World War, the British film industry produced many films about that war – and occasionally about other wars, tweaked to be reflections of the war against the Axis powers – mostly with a propagandist aim. Many were focused on the

---

[41] A phrase used several times by Richard Burton in the 1968 war movie *Where Eagles Dare*.

fortitude of the civilian population, suffering under bombing, the threat of invasion, and shortages such as rationing. It was considered vital during the war that morale not be shown to waver on screen, or to be negatively affected by material in the media, including films. Scenes or stories about the Blitz, or potential occupation, had to be couched in terms of British strength of character shining through, leading to victory over the oppressors.

Sapphire & Steel again strays into subversive territory here, when Tully, for example, is understandably appalled on behalf of Pearce when Steel questions the ghost. 'Can't you see he's a soldier?' The assumption of both heroism and moral values – honesty/honour/truthfulness based on Pearce's uniform – leads to a dangerously erroneous assumption on Tully's part, and, initially, also on Sapphire's. Assuming Pearce's truthfulness, and that he cannot be malevolent, is the trick played even on Sapphire's acute super-senses.

Film and television, however, prefer to mythologise history, and turn what was once real into mere symbolism. They are a useful tool to do so more simply, and they are very effective, because they use all the senses to transmit their transformative signal, some easily discernible, others more subliminal. Below the threshold, tunnelling under the wire between one state and another...

As the war ended, and austerity bit hard during the rebuilding of the country in the 1950s, the stories of fortitude and keeping cheerful in the face of adversity remained a popular theme, joined more frequently by dramatisations of events that occurred in the war[42]. In the 1960s and 1970s there was a spate of more action-oriented films, whether based upon real events or not, including

---

[42] In classic films such as *The Cruel Sea* (1953), *The Colditz Story* (1954), *The Dam Busters* (1955), Reach for The Sky (1956), *Ice Cold in Alex* (1958), and *Sink the Bismarck!* (1960).

Mosquito Squadron (1969), in which Steel himself – well, David McCallum – gets an earlier chance to play scenes in flying jacket and stricken aircraft.

Almost every watching in 1980 would have grown up with those old war films as regular Sunday afternoon or evening fare, usually on the BBC, throughout the 1970s.

In these films, especially post-war, but even those made during the conflict, characters could, and did, die. Soldier characters were killed in action, while civilian deaths brought pathos when the news reached the boys at the front line. But these were always what Steel refers to as 'expected' deaths. Soldiers die in battle; civilians are killed in bombings.

What is less 'expected' in the context that Steel means is that death in war, more perhaps than in any other situation, can come out of nowhere, as a random congruence of person and event completely separate from any known and accepted risk. A soldier in a war might be killed after an armistice. Civilian workers could be killed in a random street accident. These things happened – in Pearce's case, for instance, it takes time for word of the cessation of hostilities to reach units out on the front – but they tended to be frowned on by the censors.

Even in Hollywood, the first major American film to explicitly base characterisation around the issue of soldiers killed after the end of the war, was *The Big Red One* in 1980, just as *Assignment* Two was airing[43]. It's highly unlikely that the producers of either that film or

---

[43] There had been occasional films of use post-armistice death as a finale shock to the audience – 1930's *All Quiet on The Western Front*, for example – but that type of use, ending a film, avoided having the issues affect the characters. And, in the case of *All Quiet*, the ending was replaced in 1939 with an ending showing Nazis burning books, including the novel upon which the film was based.

Sapphire & Steel were aware of each other's developments, so the synchronicity of their themes is interesting. The film is based on some of director Samuel Fuller's wartime experiences, but the **Sapphire & Steel** serial is geared to simply taking the viewer in a different direction than would have been expected by the audience.

Significantly, every year on Remembrance Sunday in the United Kingdom there's a two-minute silence to mark the moment of the Armistice that ended the Great War, and the Festival of Remembrance on the previous night remains a firm fixture in the British TV schedule, so British audiences also have, along with those old war films, a culturally ingrained viewing setting for the more thoughtful and less escapist marking of the fallen in wartime. And because the Remembrance weekend is centred on Armistice Day, on the end of the First World War, it means the audience has a slightly different – more sombre and sympathetic – view of, and interaction with, media about that war. Making Private Pearce a Second World War veteran would, therefore, have had a very different feel for British audiences.

Assignment Two wasn't alone in looking seriously at the general horrors of war in its period, however. The Second World War was explored more realistically and controversially in the late 70s by series such as **Secret Army** (1977-79) on the BBC, and **Family at War** (1970-1972) and **Enemy at the Door** (1978-1980) on ITV, but this serial makes some interesting choices less often seen in other productions.

Besides the decision to make Pearce one of the resentful dead from the First World War, the serial also stresses the youth of the soldiers. The legal age for joining the British Army in 1914 was 19 but according to official figures, 250.000 boys under that age signed up, the youngest only 12.

The original ending was restored in the 1990s.

Pearce was in school and in love with his teacher, who was twelve years older than him, according to dialogue from Eleanor (the teacher) speaking through Sapphire, in *Assignment Two*. The school leaving age in 1914 was twelve, and it was raised to fourteen in 1918[44] so, depending on how long he served before dying in November of that year, he might have been sixteen or seventeen when he is killed – possibly even younger. That said, Eleanor also mentions the age gap not mattering so much when he grew up (and went to France), so possibly he was 20 or so. The ambivalence leaves a particularly interesting and chilling implication. (Or, in fact two, given the teacher-pupil dynamic.)[45]

All the soldiers are also other ranks, the history of whom had not been widely examined. History in the 1970s was still the place of great men, great deeds and great events, rather than underage boy soldiers and civilian contractors such as the submarine crew; speaking of whom, Tully is actually wrong when he says there were no civilian crew in the Second World War, the series here directly addresses a piece of missing history.

Although it has been claimed that the accident which befell HMS *Thetis* on June 29 1938 was the inspiration for this element of the episode, a similar accident involving civilian contractors aboard during sea trials is a better fit for **Sapphire & Steel**'s doomed submariners. On January 29th 1917, HMS *K13*, a steam propelled K Class submarine, was flooded due to incorrectly closed openings in its hull. In this incident, unlike the *Thetis*, the men trapped inside were able to communicate with divers outside by knocking on the hull. A little less than half of those on *K13* died, however, and the survivors were able to tell of their experiences. Adding to the

---

[44]'Extending Education, 1914-39'

[45] A youngster like Pearce is the reality behind the character Willy McBride in the haunting Eric Bogle tune, 'No Man's Land' (aka 'The Green Fields of France'). 'Well I see by your gravestone you were only 19/when you joined the great fallen of 1916'.

possible inspirations is HMS *Affray*, lost with all hands in 1950. The wife of a fellow submariner saw the image of a soaked naval officer telling her (correctly, as it turned out) where *Affray* could be found. Any or all of those – and other submarine incidents from other nations – could be the inspiration for the trapped civilian contractors, and their spectral appearance, in this story[46].

The serial here also reflects another kind of battle, as well as the trench warfare that Private Pearce knew – the battle of Religion versus Science. Again, the show offers us no reassurances, only uncomfortable questions: the souls lifted from time go back to the moment of death, but there is no mention of an afterlife; they are not souls in the sense Tully or his spiritualist church assume. Death and the threshold to life is the ultimate liminality: the one in this age more scientifically examined, the other a complete unknown. Sapphire's acknowledgement that the persona survives significantly is not placed in any context of belief.

Nevertheless, there's a definite tension between Tully's rather genteel use of bits of string, tape recordings, and Christian faith, and Steel's rationalist disdain for both his outdated equipment and his rather naive trust in an omniscient supernatural being watching over all. This, of course, is doubly ironic since Sapphire and Steel are themselves supernatural beings watching over time and dealing with problems. There's an old saying that 'we have seen the enemy and he is us,' and this is a subtle and ingenious metatextual take on that.

For a final conflict, there is the matter of Campbell's monomythical 'confrontation with the father (or authority figure),' most popularly (and literally) exemplified by Luke Skywalker and Darth Vader in the movie **Star Wars**. On the BBC, children's programming addressed the matter of conflict between rebellious youth and conventional

---

[46] Hamilton-Paterson, James, *Seven-Tenths: The Sea and Its Thresholds* (1992)

authoritarian wisdom in the likes of **Grange Hill** (1978-2008), trying to strike a careful balance of being encouraging of youthful development, but not too encouraging of rebelliousness.

CHAPTER 5: 'COME ON; YOU WANT TO SEE YOUR GHOST AGAIN?'

Steel poses this question to Tully, while setting him up for a nasty surprise, and it's a sensible thing to ask a Briton, because the ghost story is such an integral part of British culture. In fact, it's a large factor in Anglophone culture overall – and there's a reason for that.

Modern Anglophone audiences tend to associate ghost stories with Victorian – or perhaps Edwardian – times, because we think of Gothic fiction, Hammer films, and the traditional Christmas spirits of M.R. James and Charles Dickens, but the ghost story is considerably older; older even than the ghost of Hamlet's father, or Banquo, stalking the battlements of Shakespeare's historical castles.

The ghost story has its own rules and strictures, and often has a culture-specific format and structure. There's more to being a ghost story than simply being a story that happens to have a ghost in it. In fact, technically, the traditional ghost story doesn't even need to have a literal ghost in it; in form and structure, Edgar Allan Poe's *The Tell-tale Heart* hits all the ghost story's identifying marks – there's a message, unfinished business, and justice to be served, among others – yet there isn't a ghost in it. Conversely, Shakespeare's *Hamlet* has a ghost in a major role that tilts the plot, but that play is certainly not what people would call a ghost story, as the ghost is really merely a speaking character as witness.

So, what is a ghost story, and why is it such a long-lived and vital part of Britain's cultural heritage? At its base, of course, is the universal human hope for the survival of some part of the self after death. As you might expect, a belief in ghosts – and the existence of folklore and stories about them – is not a uniquely British thing. Every culture has had tales of ghosts, and every culture has their own form of fiction about meetings of mortal man with spiritual ancestor – for good or for ill. There's something different about the British ghost story, however. It's at the centre of what much of the world – not just the Anglophone world, thanks to exports and translations of Dickens and many films and TV shows – think of when they think of the phrase 'a ghost story,' and there are solid historical reasons why that is so.

However, obviously ghost stories have been around as long as there have been people[47]. We can be pretty confident that, a hundred thousand years ago, people told ghost stories around campfires. They wouldn't have called them ghost stories, of course, as the word ghost itself comes from the Old English word *gást*, which, like the German *geist* derives from the Indo-European *ghoisdos*, which meant *fury* or *anger*. In Old Norse this became a verb, *geisa*, meaning to rage, and the Norse words for ghosts are very different (*andi* and *ond*, depending on the gender of the ghost).

Why did the word for rage and fury become the word for a spirit of the dead from proto-German, down through Saxon to English, but remained simply the word for rage in Norse? Possibly because the original meaning was an animating urge of the mind, or spirit, driving both the body and the consciousness. In early pre-Germanic folklore, the dead were conducted and guided in the afterlife by the leader of the Wild Hunt, who was often referred to as the Lord of Fury. So, there was an early connection between the animus of the dead, and the emotions of fury and anger.

This word for the furious driving force of both the living person and the dead also became used as a synonym for the Latin spiritus,

---

[47] The written ghost story goes back to Pliny the Younger's story of a man named Athenodorus discovering that his house was so cheap because it was haunted by a chain-rattling ghost – a story written in 83AD.

meaning breath or blast – a sharp exhalation – from around the 9th century. In this context, however, it didn't just mean that rather excitable animal drive, but denoted any more than, or different than, human spirit or entity, regardless of whether that entity be good or evil. Demons, angels, and anything else not a mortal man could be spirit or gast; a ghost (or occasionally ghast, hence ghastly) to the rest of us. Going back to the natures of Sapphire and Steel, however, we might do well to remember that Air is a traditional element; the Roundheads may not be ghosts as Rob first thought, but they could indeed be gasts, and certainly, by not being mortal humans, come under the original meaning of spirits. In this they would also fit the Dickensian definition of spirits in *A Christmas Carol* (1843), which features both the deceased and anthropomorphised representations of concepts such as the year past, Need and Want, and other demi-religious entities under the name 'Spirits.' (For bonus points it also includes ghosts as recordings).

Between the 12th and 14th Centuries, the word ghost evolved, becoming more commonly used to refer to the discrete or discarnate soul of a deceased person appearing to the living. The reason for this is also the reason why a certain type of ghost becomes culturally significant in Britain, France, and other parts of Europe – the codification of the concept of Purgatory. Purgatory, to the medieval mind, was a place of purifying fire through which some of the dead had to pass in order to ascend to Heaven, rather than be cast into the eternally consuming fire of Hell. Unlike Heaven and Hell, though, Purgatory was thought to be a physical place on Earth, and it was believed that people – living and dead – could simply walk into and out of it.

The English and Norman medieval ghost stories and beliefs increasingly diverged from the Norse and Classical styles, to become Christian/catholic morality/propaganda pieces about the importance of prayers for the dead, interceding to let them reach heaven, and keep them from wandering out of Purgatory and around the countryside.

 As a result, these apparitions of the dead remained solid, not insubstantial. They were literally walking corpses – like those in a modern zombie movie – who could escape from Purgatory. Orderic Vitalis, who died in 1140, wrote in his eighth chronicle the tale of a knight on New Year's Day of 1091 who meets an army of the dead in Normandy. The knight encountered a column of riders, foot-soldiers, and camp followers, dozens or even hundreds strong, and he knew they were dead because he had fought with some of them, one was his brother, and he had seen some of them die. The form of this marching column of not just soldiers but their followers is visibly echoed in *Assignment Two*, with the scenes in its latter episodes of a queue of the dead waiting on the platform to be taken back to the realm of the living – just as Orderic's column of the dead had marched out of Purgatory.

Also linking the two queues of ghosts is the fact that the knight in Orderic's chronicle almost gets taken along with the dead – until his late brother recognises him and intervenes – just as both Sapphire and Steel are given a taste of the dead's deaths, and Sapphire is enfolded into the queue of the dead waiting on the platform. It's not explicitly stated, but if you're paying attention you can deduce that the dead are gathering for a journey leaving from the 'Up' platform – it's the opposite one from the platform that Steel refers to as the 'Down' platform in the first episode – which is quite telling: these dead are hoping to travel upwards, the traditional route to Heaven once freed from Purgatory, rather than downwards to Hell. And what have these dead been doing in Purgatory? Not being purified, of course, but instead being twisted by the Darkness, and driven to anger over their resentment; there are those original meanings of the words that would become what we would eventually call ghosts, again.

These are, in fact, the deepest, ghostliest of ghosts.

These substantial ghosts also do echo the ones – the Andi and the Ond – in Norse mythology who go to Hel, but sometimes turn up uninvited elsewhere and have to be put on trial for trespassing. Which is essentially what Steel seems to think his job is here. Norse ghosts were very different from the Graeco-Roman ghosts, who tended to be markers and guardians of unconsecrated burials and/or treasure hoards – something that would only come to the British ghost story after the Renaissance.

The specific kind of ghost story we think of as 'a ghost story,' especially in the Anglophone world, is a particular type of tale, with a particular structure and set of features, which really coalesced into its dominant form in the 19th Century.

The basic nature of this type of story is one in which the living encounter a supernatural being, usually an apparition of a dead person, or a set of circumstances related to the dead or the supernatural, which seeks to carry on unfinished business from a past era. This business is twofold: first, to deliver some kind of message – either to make a revelation, provoke vengeance, or otherwise convey something to the more contemporary character that the ghost could not have done while alive; and secondly, to give a stark and chilling warning to the present that the dead that have gone before are still able to affect them, for good or for ill.

In stories where the ghost or spectre is malevolent, there's still that element of it feeling hard done by. Where the ghost is guarding something – as in M.R. James' *A Warning to the Curious*, *The Treasure of Abbot Thomas*, and even *Oh Whistle, and I'll Come To You, My Lad* – it can be said to be doing a just job against potential thieves.

This vengeful – or at least ill-tempered – tone to the British ghost story is possibly partially the result of a subtle undercurrent in much of British history of being rightly afraid that the supposed condemnation of the dead would be transformed into actual condemnation by the law. This isn't just because people are often unsettled by facing their own mortality, or their being afraid of what happens to them after death. Naturally there is a certain element of that in the mix but the ghosts we love so much in literature, films and TV can actually look back with pride on the fact that the dead really did used to come back and make the living pay for their sins in Britain.

No other country in the world had quite the same system as Britain, and though it is a stretch it could be one reason why the traditional British ghost story, much later, developed the traditional elements that it did. Basically, at certain points in British history, the dead really did point the way to justice. Not in a forensic sense, but in the quite literal sense that corpses were allowed – and, indeed, encouraged – to testify in court. In some parts of the country, from 14th Century England to 17th Century Scotland, the corpse of a murder victim would be brought to the court to face the person accused of the crime. The corpse would be pricked with a knife, and the accused would be made to touch or press the corpse. If it bled, then the accused was guilty.

Obviously, this type of bizarre court procedure has long-since fallen into disuse, and was pretty much consciously forgotten even by the time of the classic British ghost story writers in the 19th century; the last case of a corpse-bleeding trial was in East Lothian in 1685, but it was still known in Shakespeare's day, and so he used some imagination and dramatic licence to have his dead characters be able to deliver dialogue in their interactions with the other characters (which, despite the legal requirements, no-one had ever managed to get a corpse to do in court.).

There had always been a connection between transport and the otherworldly, of course; from ghost ships like the legendary *Flying Dutchman*, to preternatural – not to mention apocalyptic –

horsemen, and even the older superstitions of burying suicides and execution victims at crossroads so that they couldn't so easily make the journey home. Equally, death has long and often been seen as a journey by human societies, taking high-status deceased to the afterlife by means of transport buried with them, be it Viking longship or Egyptian chariot.

Railway stations have a particular connection with the strange, weird, otherworldly, and Fortean. The railways have a popular ghost story subgenre all to themselves, in fact. Other modes of transport have it to some degree, it's true – there are tales of phantom hitch-hikers around the world, and ghost ships, and timeslips involving aeroplanes – but the railways, in terms of both trains and stations, have a special place in the realm of the strange[48].

In Britain especially, the railways have also long had a connection on some level with death, however subconsciously. There are several possible reasons for this, and they all converge rather conveniently in an era when not just life, but also death, was becoming mechanised, and industrialised.

And yet ports and stables didn't become equated with that 'undiscovered country from whose bourn no traveller returns'[49] in the same way that railway stations have. Nor have airports or (despite the setting of *Assignment Six*) motorway services.

There are a variety of reasons for this. The famous 19th century Necropolis line that took the dead out of Waterloo's Necropolis Station to Brookwood Cemetery is one cornerstone of the mythology of railway infrastructure as strange and otherworldly. Here was a form of mass transport, and its associated public travel terminus, devoted specifically to shifting the dead in large numbers.

---

[48] See Charles Dickens' 'The Signal-Man' (1866), for instance.
[49] *Hamlet*, Act 3, Scene 1, Folio 1, 1623, adjusted for modern spelling.

A railway station for the dead is a location that sticks in the mind, whether consciously or not. The Necropolis line opened in 1854, and – after switching to a new station in 1902, as the original was in the path of an expansion of Waterloo – continued operating until it was partially demolished by a Luftwaffe bomb in 1941.

This liminality between the living and the dead, people and ghosts, arrival and departure, this world and another, and the opposite directions of travel is perfectly encapsulated in Steel's second line in *Assignment Two*: 'I am from the other side... The 'Down' platform.'

Another reason why other types of travel location haven't become familiar haunts, so to speak, may simply be because those types of travel hub didn't come along at the right time – the necessary confluence of circumstance – for the zeitgeist to allow that association to be made. Only railway stations did so, on a level not seen since castles, with whom they share a certain commonality in terms of being hauntable places: both are types of structure that have endured through changing periods, and both were a type of travel hub as, in military terms, castles were essentially the equivalent of stationary aircraft carriers, from which knights and men at arms, rather than jet bombers, could be sent out to project power to surrounding areas.

The railways in Britain followed hot on the tracks – iron tracks, of course, always a metal with special significance to those concerned with the Elementals anthropomorphised as Elves and the like, to whom iron is anathema – of the stationary machines of the Industrial Revolution, which had seen resistance from those who opposed and protested the mechanical replacement of peoples' livelihoods. The railways were a sign of a more basic liminality, dividing two discrete sections of time, pre and post mechanised society, in a way that doesn't happen with the arrival or ships, cars, or aircraft. As societies became mechanised, and that mechanisation spread by rail, so too did warfare, leading to the industrialisation of killing en masse.

America already had trains co-existing with warfare in the Civil War of 1861-65, but that war was on the cusp between Napoleonic-era battlefield order and the age of the automatic weapon. Troops were still largely moved to areas of battle by foot, by horse, and by barge. In Europe, fifty years later, the train took a whole generation to the slaughter.

In both the First and Second World Wars, trains were a major logistical cornerstone for ferrying troops to the battlefronts. In particular, where Britain was concerned, conscripts first left home on trains to go to their training postings. In the First World War especially, rural stations on call-up days would have been packed with the men of their towns. In that war, Britain unwisely kept conscripts from the same towns together, making town regiments, in the belief that it would engender war-winning solidarity. In fact, of course, it meant that regiments that suffered heavy losses would all be from the same towns, meaning that whole generations of men from some areas were all but wiped out.

This lesson was learned by the time the Second World War broke out, and in terms of liminal transport, more use was made of trucks and aircraft. The association of railways and loss, however, was already firmly made. Subconsciously in the national psyche, perhaps, but solidly present. This makes the setting doubly apt for *Assignment Two*, where the resentment of the unjustly-dead is centred primarily upon a First World War soldier.

Additionally, time and different eras tend to be blended around railway stations and buildings, more than they are around other types of travel terminus. Buildings at docks and ports are often knocked down, redeveloped, or built anew; airports are constantly modernised, motorway service stations are rebuilt or expanded, and turned into entirely new out-of-town retail centres. Railways, however, are different. They may get their tracks and points and power updated, or get new engines and rolling stock, and they certainly get new computerised departure boards, but in most cases the original old building remains. It may be entirely kept or held at the heart of a new expanded station, nestled safely inside, or even repurposed as something else if the rail service has passed them by, but by and large they remain.

Of all buildings, they seem designed to fit with the ethos of the series, being places where the old mixes with the new in uncontrolled and unexpected fashions. Go to the most modern part of St Pancras, up to the top floor where Eurostar travellers get on trains heading to the north of England, and the ultra-modern chrome and glass covering rests upon Victorian stonework, with alcoves containing church-like doors that may or may not still lead to rooms or passageways.

It shouldn't be at all surprising, then, that the kinds of ghosts that Tully think he's dealing with have been a cornerstone of slow-news-day tabloids, the *Fortean Times*, and a founding target of the Society for Psychical Research since the globes of schoolrooms were covered in Imperial pink.

Crewe, for example, like several other stations, has organised ghost tours, to show off the supposed haunts of phantom cats, children's footprints that appear from nowhere (old photographs, perhaps) and even Queen Victoria herself, in a haunted lift. Carlisle Station, likewise, according to the town's own tourist website, is said to be haunted by a small boy, a veiled woman, and a headless man. (This latter, surprisingly, is actually a remarkable rarity among ghost sightings.) Smaller former stations aren't exempt: Maldon, near Chelmsford has a 'White Lady' first seen in 1958 on platform two – it's worth noting that Sapphire-as-Eleanor in *Assignment Two* wears white – which is still seen even though the station closed in 1964 and its building is now a pub.[50]

If there are such things as 'stone tape' ghosts, recordings of previous people or their souls, or the electrical pattern of their brains, then old buildings are where you'd expect to find them. In **Sapphire & Steel** we find that structures in which the old and the new are thoroughly blended are where time gets muddled, where weird and unpleasant stuff happens. If you have a message, or a recording, this is how you get interference in it, by chopping and changing the medium the message uses as a vector, or which the recording is stored upon. Stories evolve in much the same way, and so do memes, so why not messages from beyond the grave?

It's not simply that railway stations are liminal places on so many different levels, but that they are layers of different levels of liminality. They straddle then, and then, and then, and now, and in each of those they also divide home from away, past from future, life from death, point A from point B...

If elemental agencies were looking for locations designed to be fractal nests of discrete potential doorways in every conceptual direction, they'd be hard put to find a better one than a good old railway station.

---

[50] Peyton, Richard, *The Ghost Now Standing on Platform One* (1990)

CONCLUSION: 'I'D RATHER GO BACK; GO BACK FOR GOOD AND ALL'

Every journey is a story, a progression from one situation to another, or one state of being to another, and we tend to hope that the stories we experience in reality are less stressful than the stories we choose to experience in fiction.

A TV series is certainly a journey, a single serial even more so. *Assignment Two*, of course, is particularly replete with the mixture of story and journey. It is set in a railway station; it's about the arrivals and departures at a travel terminus; it's about travellers completing both their story and their journey, whether they realise and accept it or not.

This shouldn't really come as a surprise, since ghost stories are a natural type of journey story; everyone makes at least one final journey, and so it's perhaps unsurprising that there are stories of the return journey being made (or at least attempted), whether they be coming from the Up or the Down platforms...

In Campbell's monomyth, the return from the adventure is the most difficult part of all, but most rewarding. Campbell described the travel to adventure where 'a hero... crosses a threshold from the world of the everyday to a realm of adventure. Fabulous forces are encountered and a decisive victory is won. The hero returns with the power to bestow boons on his fellow man.'[51] **Sapphire & Steel** undercuts this, with only Rob and Helen making something close to the traditional journey.

Rob and Helen don't cross any threshold, however; the threshold, the journey, comes to them at home, while Tully in *Assignment*

---

[51] Campbell, *Thousand Faces*, p.23.

Two, goes to investigate a threshold. When the otherworld retreats, it leaves Rob and Helen safely in a restored normality, with the boon received of their parents' return, and perhaps eyes more open to a wider world. Tully, of course, is far less fortunate. As Shakespeare's words warn those who would explore and investigate that undiscovered country, Tully does not return.

Childhood, as we grow older, is inclined increasingly to become memories of a 'golden age' when everything was safer and better. So, we come full circle again. The interaction of nursery bogeymen and adult fears, rational education and irrational terror, combine in any age to create a very real entity in myth and fiction, and now on screen. The bogeyman, child snatcher, ogre who devours, has been around as long as we have, certainly as long as our representations of ourselves in tales, and as a mask of the Jungian Shadow. It is always an expression of the faceless, dangerous world yet overcome; a chance to learn more of ourselves and our capabilities. Rob and Helen are at an age at which even if belief in the bogeyman is fading, obedience to authority is still an important part of their lives.

This applies as much to parental authority as it does to the communal and temporal authorities such as the local policeman in whom Rob puts so much faith and whose position Steel so casually usurps. Helen is still at an age where there are stories at bedtime, Rob is on the threshold to puberty and the beginnings of adult independence, but still treated very much as a child. He begins very quickly to resent Steel, then challenge him, and eventually accept and work with him — all conflicts you could imagine him working through with his own father. In fact, all are stages of the traditional Campbell monomyth. With Steel's aid and antagonism and frequently, Sapphire's encouragement to think for himself, Rob crosses his threshold to the very beginnings of adulthood and helps save the day and solve the situation, as all of mankind has done before him, not just as a monomythical hero, but also as a rational thinker.

If the pair of elemental Operators leave any legacy with the two children, it's probably more a stock of nightmares than a sense of wonder. They also leave legacies both with the audience, and on the genre in the decades since they first materialised on our screens. In terms of memorable moments for the audience, *Assignment One* gave us Roundheads intent on murder, a haunted house full of ticking clocks, eerie voices reciting rhymes over and over, while *Adventure Two* filled our nightmares with perhaps the most widespread and lasting image of all: the empty staring black eyes belonging to a possessed heroine, and no-one able to help her. That's not the limit of the second serial's wider legacy, though.

It's appropriate that a series which is so imbued with the folklore and mythology of the past has itself been granted a lasting influence on the genre and medium of film and TV – and one which ties in to another familiar element of the human psyche and its creative works. From the folklore that the eyes were windows to the soul, and the fear of blindness, through to E.T.A Hoffmann's 'The Sandman' (1816), messing with the eyes has long been a way to instil horror in an audience.

In episode 5 of *Assignment One*, Time, or the Things dwelling in it also possess Rob's mother, revealing that this happened through the medium of her blank, staring eyes, larger than human orbs, painted on to her closed lids. In *Assignment Two*, however, the Darkness adds a new trope to that for future generations.

Black eyes, with no white, no iris, no pupil, have been subsequently used to represent possession and violation in a host of other properties, from telepaths in **Babylon 5**, and on to the alien 'black oil' parasite in **The X Files**, and are still with us in 2018 (in the BBC's **Requiem**[52], for instance). It started here in *Assignment Two*. That

---

[52] Though in **Requiem**, the actress has the luxury of staring into a mirror while the effect is added by CGI afterwards. There was no such luxury for Joanna Lumley, just extremely painful contact

was the first screen use of the trope, and perhaps it's one of the reasons – along with the performances, atmosphere, and ultimate ending – why **Sapphire & Steel** in general, and *Assignment Two* in particular, have stood the test of time so well, even if some of those who saw it only have vague memories of 'the railway station one.'

---

lenses, which she couldn't even see through.

Bibliography

Books

Auden, Wystan Hugh, 'September 1, 1939' and 'As I Walked Out One Evening, in *Another Time* (1940). Reprint, London, Faber and Faber, 2007. ISBN 9780571234370.

Bhabha, Homi K., *The Location of Culture*. New York, Routledge, 1994. ISBN 9780415336390.

Blackmore, Susan, *The Meme Machine* (1981). Reprint Oxford, Oxford University Press (1999). ISBN 9780192862129.

Butler, Elsie, *The Myth of the Magus* (1948). Reprint Cambridge, Cambridge University Press (1993). ISBN 9780521437776.

Callaghan, Richard, *Assigned! The Unofficial and Unauthorised Guide to Sapphire & Steel*. Prestatyn, Telos Publishing (2010). ISBN 9781845830328.

Cocker, Mark and Richard Mabey, *Birds Britannica*. London, Chatto & Windus (2005). ISBN 9780701169077.

Campbell, Joseph, *The Hero with a Thousand Faces*. (1949). Reprint Princeton, Princeton University Press (1972). ISBN 9780691017846.

Cornell, Paul, Day, Martin and Keith Topping, *The Guinness Book of Classic British TV* (1993). London, Guinness World Records Limited (2nd Revised Edition, 1996). ISBN 9780851125435.

Dawkins, Richard, *The Selfish Gene*. Oxford, Oxford University Press (1976). ISBN 9780199291151.

Hamilton-Paterson, James, *Seven-Tenths: The Sea and Its Thresholds*. London, Faber and Faber (1992). ISBN 9780571229383.

Harpur, Patrick, *Daimonic Reality: A Field Guide to the Otherworld* (1995). Reprint Ravensdale, Pine Winds Press 1994. ISBN 9780937663097.

Opie, Iona and Peter Opie, *The Oxford Dictionary of Nursery Rhymes* (1951). Reprint Oxford, Oxford University Press (1998). ISBN 9780198600886.

Peyton, Richard (ed.), *The Ghost Now Standing on Platform One*. London, Futura Publications (1990). ISBN 9780708849972.

Sperber, Dan, *Explaining Culture, A Naturalistic Approach*. London, Blackwell (1996). ISBN 9780631200451.

Strapalora, Giovan Francesco, *The Facetious Nights of Straparola* (1550). Reprint Wokingham, Dodo Press (2010). ISBN 9781409979517.

Umland, Samuel J. and Rebecca A. Umland, *The Use of Arthurian Legend in Hollywood Film: From Connecticut Yankees to Fisher Kings*. Westport, Praeger Publishers (1996). ISBN 9780387502588.

Vallee, Jacques, *Passport to Magonia: From Folklore to Flying Saucer.*, Daily Grail Publishing (2014). ISBN 9780987422484.

Warner, Marina, *No Go the Bogeyman: Scaring, Lulling and Making Mock*. New York City, Farrar, Straus and Giroux (1998). ISBN 9780374223014.

Zipes, Jack, *The Brothers Grimm: From Enchanted Forests to the Modern World*. London, Palgrave Macmillan (2002). ISBN 9780312293802.

Periodicals

Dunning, Stephen, 'Criticism and the "Young Adult Novel"' in *The High School Journal*, Vol. 45, No. 5 (February 1962), pp. 208-213.

Fortean Times
      #366, May 2018.
      #367, June 2018.

Television

Arthur C Clarke's World of Strange Powers. Yorkshire Television, 1985.
      Things That Go Bump in The Night.

Requiem. BBC, 2018.

The Stone Tape. BBC, 1972.

The X-Files. Fox, 1993-2002, 2016-2018

Film

Milestone, Lewis, dir, *All Quiet on The Western Front.* Universal Pictures, 1930.

Web

'Doppelgänger'. https://www.britannica.com/art/doppelganger. Accessed 8 July 2018.

Clark, Finn, 'Sapphire and Steel: Assignment 1'. http://finnclark.thiswaydown.org/Review/SapphireandSteelAssignment1.html. Accessed 8 July 2018.

Cult TV Lounge, 'Sapphire and Steel, Assignments One to Four'. http://cult-tv-lounge.blogspot.com/2014/05/sapphire-and-steel-assignments-one-to.html. Accessed 8 July 2018.

'Extension of education, 1914-39', https://www.parliament.uk/about/living-heritage/transformingsociety/livinglearning/school/overview/1914-39/. Accessed 8 July 2018.

Leon, Melissa, 'Gillian Anderson: I Was Offered Half Duchovny's Pay for 'The X-Files' Revival', *Daily Beast*, 22 January 2016. https://www.thedailybeast.com/gillian-anderson-i-was-offered-half-duchovnys-pay-for-the-x-files-revival. Accessed 8 July 2018.

Phillips, Steve, 'Andy's Anachronisms -- Time Travel Television Reviews 'Sapphire and Steel'. http://www.timetravelreviews.com/tv_reviews/sapphire_steel.html Accessed 8 July 2018.

'Post-traumatic stress disorder (PTSD)'. https://www.nhs.uk/conditions/post-traumatic-stress-disorder-ptsd/symptoms/. Accessed 8 July 2018.

Vitalis, Ordericus, *The Ecclesiastic History of England and Normandy*. https://archive.org/download/ecclesiasticalhi01ordeuoft/ecclesiasticalhi01ordeuoft_djvu.txt. Accessed 8 July 2018.

Biography

David McIntee is a novelist, who has written both original fiction and tie-in works for many of the largest franchises in television and movies.

Lesley McIntee graduated from the University of Manchester in 2011 with an MPhil on the figure of the Magus and the creative artist in German Romanticism. She has a lifelong interest in history of the occult, alchemy, myth and folklore.